MICROSOFT® EXCHANGE
SERVER™ 5.5

Patrick Grote

in 10 Minutes

SAMS

A Division of Macmillan Computer Publishing
201 West 103rd St., Indianapolis, Indiana, 46290 USA

Sams Teach Yourself Microsoft® Exchange Server™ 5.5 in 10 Minutes

Copyright © 1999 by Sams Publishing

All rights reserved. No part of this book shall be reproduced, stored in a retrieval system, or transmitted by any means, electronic, mechanical, photocopying, recording, or otherwise, without written permission from the publisher. No patent liability is assumed with respect to the use of the information contained herein. Although every precaution has been taken in the preparation of this book, the publisher and author assume no responsibility for errors or omissions. Neither is any liability assumed for damages resulting from the use of the information contained herein.

International Standard Book Number: 0-672-31556-4

Library of Congress Catalog Card Number: 98-89637

Printed in the United States of America

First Printing: March 1999

01   00   99   4   3   2   1

EXECUTIVE EDITOR
Grace Buechlein

DEVELOPMENT EDITOR
Gregory Harris

MANAGING EDITOR
Brice Gosnell

PROJECT EDITOR
Gretchen Uphoff

COPY EDITOR
Pamela Woolf

PROOFREADER
Andrew Beaster

INDEXER
Eric Schroeder

TECHNICAL EDITOR
Matthew Gillard

PRODUCTION
Brandon Allen
Stacey DeRome
Timothy Osborn

TRADEMARKS

All terms mentioned in this book that are known to be trademarks or service marks have been appropriately capitalized. Sams Publishing cannot attest to the accuracy of this information. Use of a term in this book should not be regarded as affecting the validity of any trademark or service mark. Microsoft is a registered trademark of Microsoft Corporation. Exchange Server is a trademark of Microsoft Corporation.

WARNING AND DISCLAIMER

Every effort has been made to make this book as complete and as accurate as possible, but no warranty or fitness is implied. The information provided is on an *as is* basis. The author and publisher shall have neither liability nor responsibility to any person or entity with respect to any loss or damages arising from the information contained in this book.

CONTENTS

PART 5   ADVANCED EXCHANGE FEATURES

17   KEY MANAGEMENT SERVER   244

18   MICROSOFT EXCHANGE 5.5 FORMS   249

19   DISASTER PREVENTION   254

INDEX   261

About the Author

Patrick Grote's Microsoft Exchange experience began with a foundation of Microsoft Mail and grew with hands-on experience with each version of Microsoft Exchange. With more than 10 years of networking and email experience, combined with Microsoft Certified Systems Engineer status, Patrick sports the experience and knowledge necessary to write an authoritative book on Microsoft Exchange Server 5.5.

Being a writer for most of his professional life, Patrick authored his own shareware reviews before most people knew the concept of shareware. His three years as a managing editor of a regional computing newspaper allows him to bring the wonderful world of Microsoft Exchange 5.5 to readers in plain and simple language. You'll be able to put the knowledge of this book to work for you immediately.

DEDICATION

We owe who we are to our parents. This book is dedicated to Bill and Mary Grote. Finer parents have never existed.

ACKNOWLEDGMENTS

As I assumed the task of writing a book, I really didn't know what I was getting into. Without the help of people who did know what I was getting into, my efforts would have ended up as a bunch of jumbled, rambling words.

I'd like to thank Grace Buechlein, executive editor, of Macmillan Computer Publishing's Desktop Operating Systems group for offering me the opportunity to help you learn more about Microsoft Exchange 5.5. As I worked through the project, Grace was never further than an email message or a phone call away with help and guidance.

I'd like to thank Gregory Harris, development editor, for helping me beat my prose into a more focused and disciplined effort. I would read my work after Gregory tempered it with his knowledge and talent and shake my head muttering, "That's what I wanted to get across!"

When you work in the technical field and reach a certain level of competence, you come to think two things of yourself: 1) You know as much as you can about a product and 2) You can explain it to anyone. Technical editor Matthew Gillard's job was to check that I wrote for technical accuracy. You can thank him for making sure I explained certain terms and concepts to you in plain English.

In addition to the folks who masterfully pieced this book together are those people whose priorities and needs took a back seat while I was writing. There are three people I have to thank for their patience, encouragement, and guidance.

My mother-in-law, Judy Hickham, who really made an impact in my life when I accepted the challenge of writing this book. Thanks for being there for me.

My wonderfully spectacular eight-year-old daughter, Cassandra. All I have to say now is, "Yes Cassie, Daddy's office door is unlocked now and you can come in anytime you want." Thanks for helping me relax by playing ball with me between writing sessions.

Finally, I'm not a matrimony expert. I'm much better at facilitating communication between two Microsoft Exchange 5.5 sites than between a husband and wife. What I did learn throughout this process is that my wife, Melissa, truly is my soul mate. So much of the enjoyment I experience in life is because she is experiencing it with me. I'd like to thank her for the late night backrubs and the frequent soda runs. She's as much a part of this book as I am.

TELL US WHAT YOU THINK!

As the reader of this book, *you* are our most important critic and commentator. We value your opinion and want to know what we're doing right, what we could do better, what areas you'd like to see us publish in, and any other words of wisdom you're willing to pass our way.

As the executive editor for the operating systems team at Macmillan Computer Publishing, I welcome your comments. You can fax, email, or write me directly to let me know what you did or didn't like about this book—as well as what we can do to make our books stronger.

Please note that I cannot help you with technical problems related to the topic of this book, and that due to the high volume of mail I receive, I might not be able to reply to every message.

When you write, please be sure to include this book's title and author, as well as your name and phone or fax number. I will carefully review your comments and share them with the author and editors who worked on the book.

Fax: 317-581-4663

Email: opsys@mcp.com

Mail: Executive Editor
            Operating Systems
            201 West 103rd Street
            Indianapolis, IN 46290 USA

INTRODUCTION

If you've already bought this book, welcome and rest assured you've made a wonderful choice to help you learn and manage Microsoft Exchange Server 5.5.

If you're still thinking about whether to buy this book, let me give you a reason: Answers. This book is crammed with the answers you need to learn and manage Microsoft Exchange Server 5.5. I've designed the book to facilitate finding answers to your Microsoft Exchange Server 5.5 questions. The following are the top 10 support issues facing new Microsoft Exchange 5.5 administrators, and where in this book you'll find the answers.

1. Troubleshooting Email Issues: Lesson 15

2. Adding a New User: Lesson 7

3. Using Exchange Administrator: Lesson 6

4. Creating Public Folders: Lesson 12

5. Transferring Mail with Other Microsoft Exchange 5.5 Servers: Lesson 8

6. Installing Outlook 98: Lesson 7

7. How Microsoft Exchange 5.5 Works: Lesson 1

8. Backing Up Microsoft Exchange 5.5: Lesson 14

9. Troubleshooting Microsoft Exchange 5.5 Issues: Lesson 16

10. Connecting Microsoft Exchange 5.5 with the Internet: Lesson 9

If your questions are not addressed in the top 10 list, don't fret! I'll cover many more issues and concepts that you'll appreciate as a new Microsoft Exchange 5.5 administrator.

I know you are a busy person who needs Microsoft Exchange 5.5 answers fast! Like all the books in the *Sams Teach Yourself in 10 Minutes* series, I promise this one will deliver the goods to you in a language you can understand.

CONVENTIONS USED IN THE BOOK

This book uses the following conventions:

- Information you type appears in a special **boldface** type.

- Menus, buttons, and options that you click on or select appear in a **bolded blue** font.

In addition to the background information and step-by-step instructions, this book contains other useful tips, cautions, and plain English boxes, each identified with an icon.

> **Tip**   You can review these tips to find out shortcuts and other timesaving advice.

> **Caution**   Read these cautions to avoid common mistakes and potential problems.

> **Plain English**   Read these plain English boxes for explanations of new terms and definitions.

Lesson 1

General Concept

In this lesson you'll learn what makes Microsoft Exchange Server 5.5 work, the basic structure of the software and how mail is delivered.

Exchange Overview

Microsoft Exchange 5.5 is one of the more powerful, secure and robust mail servers available on the market today. Seven years in development, Microsoft crafted Exchange from the ground up, creating a very stable and high performing email and groupware server. Microsoft Exchange combines the latest technology with administrative tools to bring you full control over all aspects of your company's communications. Based on a *client/server* model, Microsoft Exchange is powerful, but can be complex to install, maintain, and troubleshoot.

 Client/Server In a client/server environment, the server processes information supplied by the client. In the Microsoft Exchange environment, this means the server is responsible for routing and distributing messages, not the client. This leads to a much more reliable and robust system.

How It Works

The inner-workings of Microsoft Exchange are handled by four distinct components. These components are as follows:

- Mail transfer agent
- Information store

- Directory services

- System attendant

A database ties all the components together, so if you think about it, Microsoft Exchange is just one large database that routes and distributes data. You can see the four components in Figure 1.1. They are described here in a little more detail.

System Attendant		
Mail Transfer Agent	Information Store	Directory Services

FIGURE 1.1   The Microsoft Exchange 5.5 components.

MAIL TRANSFER AGENT

The *Mail Transfer Agent* component is responsible for routing messages to other Microsoft Exchange servers, gateways to the other email systems (including the Internet), or other external services such as a fax or pager gateway. Commonly referred to as an MTA, this is one of the most vital components of Exchange. If the MTA is not working, you might experience one of the following problems:

- Internet mail is not being received or delivered.

- Other branches in your company are not receiving mail your branch is sending.

- Other branches in your company can not deliver mail they have queued for your branch.

- Faxes are not being routed to the fax gateway.

Troubleshooting mail delivery issues is discussed in Lesson 16, "Microsoft Exchange 5.5 Server Troubleshooting."

INFORMATION STORE

The *Information Store* (IS) is the index for Microsoft Exchange's message database. All messages and folder contents residing on a Microsoft Exchange server are contained in a message database. The IS manages the reference pointers for access and contains a list of all mail objects in each user's mailbox and public folders. Each time a message is sent, read, or deleted, the IS monitors and records its status through a transaction log. The IS then updates the pointer that references the message in the message database.

The two distinct subcomponents to the IS are public and private stores.

Public stores are used for public folders, Internet newsgroups, and other information that is not user-specific.

User-specific objects, such as email boxes, are stored in the private store. The private store also contains the user's distribution lists and custom recipients.

The Information Store is critical for maintaining an accurate database of information. If it becomes corrupt or is not functioning, some of the following issues might occur:

- Messages might disappear.

- Messages might be routed to the wrong recipient.

- Folder information might be lost.

- Attachments might disappear.

- Some Exchange services might not start or hang during startup.

Lesson 15, "Client Troubleshooting Guide," discusses solving these issues.

DIRECTORY SERVICES

The Microsoft Exchange directory service creates and manages the *directory objects*. Directory objects include users, groups, sites, and servers.

One of the unique features of Microsoft Exchange is that its Directory Services are hierarchical, so that permission to modify certain objects can be granted to specific users. For example, by using Directory Services, an email administrator can grant administrative permission to a branch manager. This allows the branch manager to modify users at the local branch, but not at other branches.

The Directory Service does more than just manage objects, it also verifies and approves requests to modify the Microsoft Exchange database. When a user attempts to modify any object, the Directory Service controls access to the object.

If the Directory Services are not functioning properly, one of the following issues might occur:

- Administration of the Microsoft Exchange server would not be possible.

- Permissions cannot be modified.

- User access might be denied when attempting to access Microsoft Exchange services.

- Object properties cannot be modified.

These issues will be demonstrated more in Lesson 16.

SYSTEM ATTENDANT

The System Attendant works to maintain the performance of the Microsoft Exchange server. As it runs on the server, the System Attendant ensures each of the other components completes their tasks. The System Attendant is responsible for many functions, including the following:

- Creation and maintenance of routing tables, which provide directions to the MTA concerning mail delivery.

- Generates Microsoft Exchange email addresses for new users.

- Generates foreign or gateway email addresses as needed. For example, Internet or fax addresses for new users.

- Monitors message connectors between Microsoft Exchange servers. This monitoring ensures the communication roadway is clear, so messages can be routed to other servers.

- Verifies and maintains directory validation on a Microsoft Exchange server.

The System Attendant is an integral part of the Microsoft Exchange infrastructure. Without it, Microsoft Exchange would not function. It would be similar to the main computer on the space shuttle failing—nothing can happen until the problem is fixed.

MAIL DELIVERY

The process of delivering mail through the Microsoft Exchange system has to be very reliable. When a client generates a message, the IS receives the message and determines the delivery method based on the addressee. The addressee information is obtained by consulting the Directory Services.

After the destination address and permissions of the user who sent the message is verified, the message is relayed to the MTA. The MTA queries the System Attendant for the most efficient route to send the message. Based on the configuration of the Microsoft Exchange server, the MTA then sends the message to the appropriate system.

As the message works its way through the Microsoft Exchange components, the System Attendant runs in the background verifying connections, ensuring directory consistency, and responding to routing table updates from the MTA.

Because of the client/server model, while this message delivery process is occurring on the server, the client that sent the message can continue to work at his or her workstation without having to wait for message delivery.

In this lesson, you covered the general concept of Microsoft Exchange as a messaging software suite. You also learned some basic ideas of how Internet and network messaging systems function. In the next lesson, you'll learn about Exchange's features and the components of the Exchange server.

LESSON 2

GENERAL
PRODUCT
FEATURES

In this lesson, you'll learn about some of the unique features of Microsoft Exchange 5.5.

EXCHANGE FEATURES

Microsoft Exchange 5.5 features some of the more advanced options you would expect from today's leading email and groupware product, including

- Internet mail connectivity

- Public folders

- Microsoft Exchange 5.5 specific monitoring tools

- Key Management

- Forms management

- Directory Replication

INTERNET MAIL CONNECTIVITY

Microsoft Exchange 5.5 supports Internet mail connectivity through its Internet Mail service. Providing both server and client connectivity, the Internet Mail service supports the common *protocols* POP3, IMAP4, and SMTP.

Protocols When an Exchange client wants to talk to a Microsoft Exchange 5.5 Server they need to do it in a common protocol. A protocol is an agreed upon method for communicating. Like a common language, a common protocol specifies the language and the format to use.

Internet Mail service supports administration of the connectivity you install, which includes permissions, routing, restrictions, and security.

You can assign permissions to users and groups so that those users and groups can handle common administration tasks, such as searching for and deleting messages themselves.

Routing configuration allows you to configure how Internet Mail Service handles incoming mail. The option to reroute incoming mail can be fully controlled.

Internet Mail Service can restrict mail delivery by limiting the size of messages being received. This feature is powerful for preventinglarge messages from consuming your Internet resources. You can also restrict mail based on the email recipient. This feature allows you to limit Internet email to those users who need it.

Internet Abuse? If you have users who do not need Internet email access, such as temporary workers or users who abuse Internet email; you can deny their ability to send Internet email. Because of the popularity of the Internet, many corporations have instituted Internet policies. Using Internet Mail Service ensures that your Internet policy is on track.

Using the Internet as a method of transferring email is quick, efficient, and reliable. Unfortunately, security is not one of the default benefits of Internet email. When email is passed through systems on the Internet, it is typically in a plain-text format, so anyone with administration rights at other sites has the ability to read these messages.

Fortunately, the Internet Mail Service offers several configuration options for ensuring your email communications remain secure.

- **No Authentication or encryption**—Email is sent in clear text form, which is readable by anyone.

- **SASL Encryption**—Simple Authentication and Security Layer provides authentication and encrypted transmission.

- **SASL/AUTH Clear Text Password Authentication**—Authenticates the connectivity password in clear text.

- **SSL Encryption**—Secure Layer Sockets allows for tight encryption for authentication and transmission.

- **Windows NT Challenge/Response Authentication and Encryption**—Uses Microsoft's standard encryption for authentication and encryption.

 Encryption   Encryption is the process of encoding data so it is unreadable.

As you can see, the Internet Mail Service is extremely powerful. The details of configuring the Internet Mail Service are in Lesson 9, "The Internet Mail Service."

PUBLIC FOLDERS

Being able to share information with people across your company or organization can be a very useful tool. Managing these common areas could pose an administration nightmare, but Microsoft Exchange 5.5 makes it easier through the use of *public folders*.

Public folders are mailbox folders that are available to everyone in your organization, but you can restrict access to the folders if you need to. Information such as mail messages, files, documents, forms, and Internet newsgroups can be accessed via public folders.

Users can submit information to a public folder in many ways, including the following:

- **Posting items to a public folder**—Creating an item in a public folder is the same as creating a mail message. You can add any information, including files and documents.

- **Addressing items to a public folder**—Public folders display as an addressee in the Global Address List (GAL). This makes it easy for a user to *CC:* an email message to the public folder as if it was a real recipient, and thereby allows you to share information. You can also use this feature to store a record of announcements or broadcast messages.

- **Drag and drop information to a public folder**—This features works great for users who want to share common programming code or HTML designs.

 CC: and BCC: In the email world, the standard term for sending a copy of a message to someone is *CC:*, an abbreviation for carbon copy. For instance, you can send a message to your boss letting her know you'll be out on Friday, and you can CC: your co-workers to let them know as well.

A *BCC:* is a blind carbon copy. On a typical carbon copy, the message recipient can see who you have sent a copy of the message to. By using the blind carbon copy, the message recipient does not see who you have sent copies to.

Public folders are an easy concept to understand, but they are very configurable. Lesson 12, "Creating and Using Public Folders," discusses them in greater detail.

THE POWER OF COLLABORATION

Public folders bring a new level of collaboration to your organization by providing common ground for users to share resources.

A perfect use of public folders can be found with any committee. Typically, committees are designed to accomplish specific goals, whether that is completing a budget, working on revenue goals, or deciding where to have the annual Christmas party.

In the case of an annual budget, each department head needs to submit specific cost estimates and numbers for review. Instead of making one individual the point person for collecting and redistributing submissions, the department heads can submit their budgets to the public folder. At this point, other department heads can review the document while the committee head can await final revisions.

SPECIFIC MONITORING TOOLS

Microsoft Exchange 5.5 is the luxury model for enterprise email solutions. Just as luxury cars have onboard sensors to report performance, Microsoft Exchange 5.5 offers similar sensors.

Microsoft Exchange 5.5 allows you to monitor server and connectivity components. Server components include items such as services and internal processes. Connectivity components include connections to other email systems and servers.

By using Microsoft Windows NT's own Performance Monitor, you can check the health of your Exchange Server by selecting default values. There are more than 100 unique counters you can monitor for Microsoft Exchange 5.5. This helps you verify any issues that occur and solve performance problems.

You can also set triggers to alert you if your Microsoft Exchange 5.5 installation develops problems. You can set the following types of alerts:

- **Screen Message**—A message pops up on the designated user's computer screen.

- **Email Message**—If possible, an email message is mailed to the designated user.

- **Process**—A program can be run in response to an alert; it could be a process to delete or compress files. The process can also send a beep or page to the administrator.

The capability to monitor every aspect of Microsoft Exchange 5.5 is critical in today's 24 hour a day, 7 day a week environment. Although it takes a concerted effort to ensure that the most important events are tracked, the efforts are well rewarded.

Monitoring is discussed in detail in Part 4, "Troubleshooting."

HEALTHY MONITORING

Just as you monitor your health through blood pressure and cholesterol screenings, you need to ensure your Microsoft Exchange 5.5 installation remains healthy as well.

Many people don't monitor performance until their Microsoft Exchange 5.5 installation starts acting wacky. Unless you have a baseline measurement of your Microsoft Exchange 5.5 installation though, you won't know where to look to try to make the situation better. A baseline of your Microsoft Exchange 5.5 installation demonstrates the performance when conditions are optimal.

By comparing your baseline to current monitoring results, you should be able to see where the problems are occurring.

KEY MANAGEMENT

If your organization requires very high security when transferring mail from one site to another, Microsoft Exchange 5.5 offers a security feature called Key Management.

Key Management uses a software-basedsent from one site to another, but your system needs a Key Management Server to enable this feature. The Key Management Server's role is to organize and manage the distribution and verification of keys.

The Key Management administrator needs access to the Microsoft Exchange 5.5 administration program because he or she handles all user requests for keys and works to ensure the system stays encrypted.

The following clients support Key Management:

- Microsoft Exchange Clients running on Windows 3.x, Windows 95, Windows NT and Macintosh

- Outlook Clients running on Windows 95 or Windows NT

No Key Management in DOS Client The Exchange MS-DOS client doesn't support the Key Management feature.

Key Management is a very powerful feature that almost guarantees your messages will be delivered securely. It is covered in more detail in Lesson 17, "Key Management Server."

ELECTRONIC SIGNATURES ARE HERE

Key Management brings more than just secure communications to your email; it also brings the ability to digitally sign documents.

If your organization relies on signatures to approve items such as purchase orders or human resource requests, you can use the features of Key Management to bring auditable documents to your organization in electronic form.

Instead of submitting a purchase request in paper form, you can now send an email message. The email message can be approved with a digital signature by the purchasing agent, and then forwarded to the vendor; the vendor would know that the purchase request is valid and can fulfill the request without generating any paper.

FORMS MANAGEMENT

Microsoft Exchange 5.5 includes many features that have been wholly embraced by the computing community. However, an extremely powerful feature that is not fully utilized is *Exchange Forms*.

Exchange Forms are screen designs used to enter input into Microsoft Exchange 5.5. A typical form is the New Message screen used to send email messages. Using Exchange Forms Designer, you can create any type of form you need.

Each Exchange form is designed with a certain goal in mind. For example, the New Message form is designed to send an email message. The information you give the form is entered in a field; these fields relate to recipient, subject, and so on. When you create your own forms, you can add completely different fields that relate to your database, employee directory, or any other information.

Microsoft Exchange 5.5 makes managing forms much easier. Through the use of an Organization Forms Library, you have complete control over the permissions and distribution attributes of a form.

You can use forms to simplify and organize your routine tasks. The following are a few examples of using forms:

- **Expense reports**—You can create an Exchange Form to handle expense reports. The form can total the amount needed, and then forward the form to the appropriate person.

- **Vacation requests**—You can make an Exchange Form for vacation or time-off requests. The form can be designed to allow a user to graphically choose the dates, and then submit the request to the appropriate person.

- **Phone messages**—You can create an Exchange Form to handle phone messages while people are out of the office. The form looks like one of those pink *While You Were Out* messages and the information can be stored in a database.

Forms Management is a very solid tool to use in your organization. By centralizing your processes through the use of Microsoft Exchange 5.5 you can save time and money.

Exchange Forms are discussed in more detail in Lesson 18, "Microsoft Exchange 5.5 Forms."

FILE THAT FORM

One of the main benefits of using Exchange Forms can be found in record keeping. Each business or organization keeps records for archival purposes, but photocopying and storing ordinary forms can be costly.

By using Exchange Forms, forms and their approval can be stored online in a standard method. This makes historical storage and retrieval much easier, saving time and money.

DIRECTORY REPLICATION

The process of replication can be thought of like cloning. Before you begin thinking that Microsoft Exchange 5.5 is going to run amok and make copies of everything, rest assured. *Directory Replication* under Microsoft Exchange 5.5 is very configurable and easy to use.

Directory Replication allows you to control where copies of items are stored, such as your GAL and pubic folders. You can replicate information on the same site or between sites.

 Replication Requires Extra Space   Keep in mind that replicated items take extra storage space on the server you replicate to. For example, if you replicate a large public folder full of graphics totaling one gigabyte in size from SERVERA to SERVERB, you will need to plan for an extra one gigabyte of space on SERVERB.

Two benefits of Directory Replication are

- **Bandwidth conservation**—By using replicated directories, a user from one site doesn't have to consult a directory at another site. This alleviates network traffic when checking a directory.

- **Fault tolerance**—If a user at one site wants to read public folders on another site, they would typically connect to the other site. If the public folder was replicated throughout the organization, all queries are done locally. The other site with the required data could be disconnected or unavailable and the user would not need to know; user access to the public folders would be available.

Using Directory Replication helps you manage your communication routes and ensure high availability of your Microsoft Exchange 5.5 resources.

GROUP COMMUNICATIONS ACROSS THE COUNTRY?

One of the more problematic aspects of working with a national company is group collaboration. Sometimes users need to brainshare and communicate with each other as a group through email. Microsoft Exchange 5.5 supports this through the use of public folders.

The biggest pitfall when using public folders in the past was the location of the public folders. In a typical organization the public folder is stored on the main corporate server. If a local branch or office is disconnected from the main office (a lost communication line), users wouldn't be able to access the public folder.

Through the use of Directory Replication a communication outage or other disconnection wouldn't affect local users. They could still reference the public folders and even change them by adding new ideas or modifying someone else's idea. When the outage is repaired, Microsoft Exchange 5.5 automatically replicates the modified information.

In this lesson, you learned about the basic features of Exchange and the components of the Exchange Server. In the next lesson, you'll learn about the various clients Exchange supports.

LESSON 3

MICROSOFT EXCHANGE 5.5 CLIENTS

In this lesson you'll learn about Outlook and the Microsoft Exchange clients. You'll also learn about the requirements to use each client and the available features.

The strength of Microsoft Exchange 5.5 lies not only in its server-based capabilities but also in the power of its clients. The clients supported by Microsoft Exchange 5.5 range from simple Internet-based email programs to advanced contact management and calendar and scheduling applications, such as Outlook 98.

The unique concept behind Microsoft Exchange 5.5 supplied clients is usability. Advanced features are available to users in an easy-to-use interface.

Today's Exchange client of choice is Outlook 98. It is extremely powerful, combining elements of an email client and a personal information manager.

There are three versions of Outlook 98:

- Outlook 98 for Windows 95/98/NT

- Outlook for Macintosh

- Outlook Web Access

Get the Current Version   There are two other versions of Outlook you should be aware of: Outlook 97 and Outlook Express. Outlook 97 is the older version of Outlook 98 and supports Microsoft Exchange 5.5. Outlook Express is the email program supplied with Internet Explorer and only supports Internet email.

Regardless of which client you choose to implement, the core functionality of Microsoft Exchange 5.5 will be available. With Microsoft Exchange 5.5's core functionality, you'll be able to complete the following tasks:

- Receive email messages
- Send email messages
- Search address books
- Remotely access email
- Store information in folders

 Outlook Not Bright for Older Exchange Clients Microsoft has stated that their future direction for accessing Microsoft Exchange 5.5 is Outlook. Further development of the Exchange client has been discontinued (except to fix major bugs). If you are considering a Microsoft Exchange 5.5 installation or migration from MS Mail, plan on using the Outlook client.

OUTLOOK—THE FUTURE OF MICROSOFT EXCHANGE 5.5 CLIENTS

Microsoft is moving away from the basic Exchange client and embracing their new Outlook application. The key to the Outlook interface is the *Inbox*, shown in Figure 3.1. The Inbox is the area where all your messages are stored when they are received. You can also send messages and configure Outlook from the Inbox.

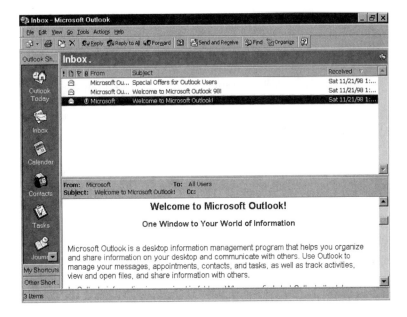

FIGURE 3.1   The Outlook Inbox.

Outlook not only allows access to the Exchange server, but also provides the following additional functionality in the Windows 95, NT, and Macintosh versions.

- **Calendar**—Outlook sports a very flexible calendar function for tracking appointments, to-do lists, and meetings. You can see the Calendar in Figure 3.2. This functionality replaces Schedule+ in the normal Exchange client.

- **Contacts**—Unlike the typical personal address book included with the Microsoft Exchange client, Outlook contains a whole section devoted to contacts, as you can see in Figure 3.3. Contact information can include the regular name, address, city, state, and ZIP, as well as more detailed information such as email addresses and birth dates. And, if Outlook doesn't provide a field you need, you can add custom fields.

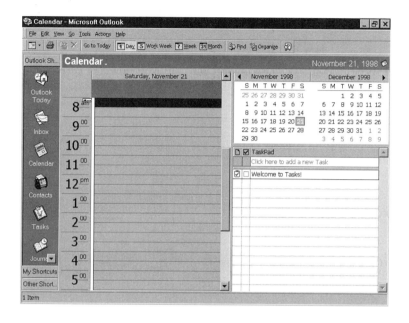

FIGURE 3.2   The Outlook Calendar function.

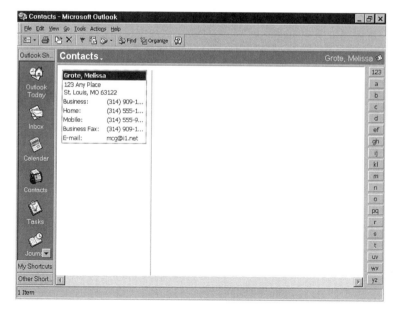

FIGURE 3.3   The Outlook Contacts function.

- **Tasks**—Everyone has a to-do list; Outlook brings that information into the email client, as shown in Figure 3.4. This allows you to assign tasks to others or check on the status of tasks from a centralized location. Tasks can be associated with contacts and audited in the journal section (which is covered next).

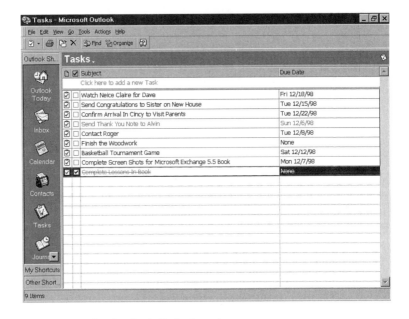

FIGURE 3.4   The Outlook Tasks function.

- **Journal**—The journal function, shown in Figure 3.5 allows you to track all correspondence to a contact from the contact database. You can track not only email messages and phone calls, but also which files you sent to a contact. The Journal feature is perfect for tracking sales calls or feedback processes.

- **Notes**—Stickies, as most of us like to call them, have become electronic. Outlook allows you to create and manipulate your own electronic sticky notes for jotting down brief bits of information. You can do neat things such as change the note color, forward to email users, and save in priority order. You can see Outlook's Notes in Figure 3.6.

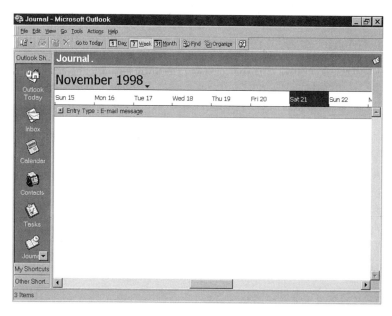

FIGURE 3.5 The Outlook Journal function.

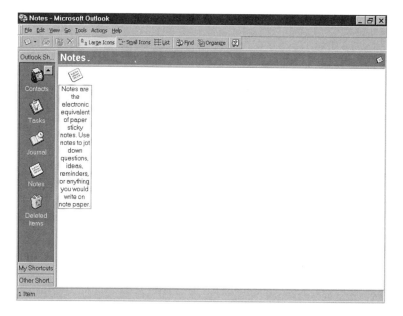

FIGURE 3.6 The Outlook Notes function.

Outlook Express is an email client bundled with Internet Explorer 4.x; it was not designed to be a full Exchange client. Supporting only basic Internet email functionality, Outlook Express can communicate with an Exchange server, but only for transferring Internet email. None of the advanced Exchange features such as scheduling, forms, folders, or address books are supported in Outlook Express.

OLDER EXCHANGE CLIENTS

Sometimes your technology (or budgetary) needs might call for using one of the older Exchange clients. This is typically true in organizations whose standard is still Windows 3.1x, or for companies that need to support MS-DOS clients.

You can still order the Microsoft Exchange 5.0 client pack, which contains the following clients:

- MS-DOS Exchange

- Windows 3.1x

- Windows 95

- Windows NT

- Windows Macintosh

MS-DOS EXCHANGE CLIENT

The MS-DOS Exchange client, shown in Figure 3.7, is a simple program and is intended for those users with limited resources who want basic email functionality.

The Versatile DOS Client   The MS-DOS client can be used with Windows NT, Windows 95, or Windows 98 in an MS-DOS box.

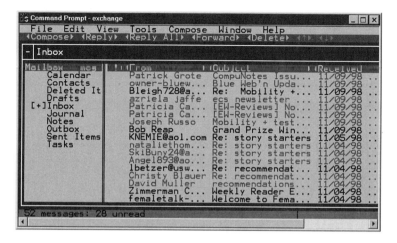

FIGURE 3.7   The MS-DOS client

The minimum requirements for using the MS-DOS client are as follows :

* MS-DOS 5.0 or higher

* 1MB of RAM

* 2MB of available hard drive space

* Network connection to the Microsoft Exchange 5.5 Server

* Modem

 Speed Trap   As always, your modem speed will directly affect the performance of Exchange. Use the fastest modem you can afford.

WINDOWS 3.1X CLIENT

The Windows 3.1x client, shown in Figure 3.8, is the first client to fully support all Exchange features. Basic and advanced features are supported in a true 16-bit application.

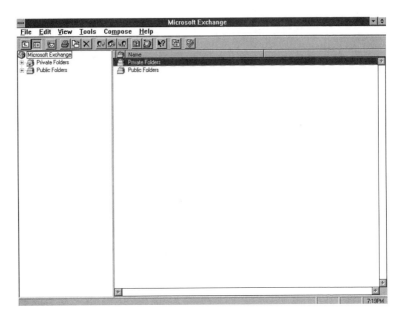

FIGURE **3.8**   The Windows 3.1x client.

To support meeting and appointment requests, the Schedule+ program is included. The Exchange Windows 3.1x client and Schedule+ work in tandem to support the time management features of Exchange.

One of the benefits of using the Windows 3.1x client is the capability to connect to an existing MS Mail and Windows for Workgroups post office. This is important if you are considering a migration from MS Mail to Exchange.

 INI Port in a Storm   The Exchange Windows 3.1x client uses old-style INI files to manage various configuration settings.

The minimum requirements for using the Windows 3.1x client are as follows:

- Windows 3.1x with networking or Windows for Workgroups
- 8MB of RAM
- 12MB of available hard drive space
- Network connection to the Microsoft Exchange 5.5 Server
- Modem

WINDOWS 95 CLIENT

The Windows 95 Exchange client, shown in Figure 3.9, is a true 32-bit application that supports all the basic and advanced features of Exchange. This client is also compatible with Windows 98.

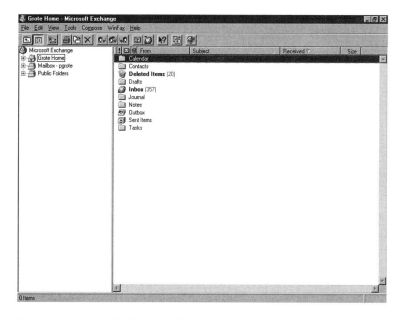

FIGURE 3.9 The Windows 95 client.

The Schedule+ program is installed by default to support meeting and appointment requests. The Exchange Windows 95 client and Schedule+ work together to support the time management features of Exchange.

As with the Windows 3.1x client, support for MS Mail and Windows for Workgroups post offices is provided. This is an excellent feature for managing a migration from MS Mail to Exchange.

Configuration information for the Exchange Windows 95 client is stored in the system Registry files (instead of the INI files used by the Windows 3.1x client).

Different user-specific information can be stored in profiles using the Exchange Windows 95 client. This makes it possible to configure the Exchange Windows 95 client to access email for multiple users on one machine. You can also use profiles to access multiple email services.

The minimum requirements for using the Windows 95 client are as follows:

- Windows 95 or Windows 98

- 8MB of RAM

- 12MB of available hard drive space

- Network connection to the Microsoft Exchange 5.5 Server

- Modem

WINDOWS NT CLIENT

The Windows NT client, like its Windows 95 counterpart, is a true 32-bit Windows NT application that supports all the basic and advanced features of Exchange. You can see the Windows NT client in Figure 3.10.

To support meeting and appointment requests, the Schedule+ program comes with the Exchange client package. The Exchange Windows NT client and Schedule+ work in concert to support the time management features of Exchange.

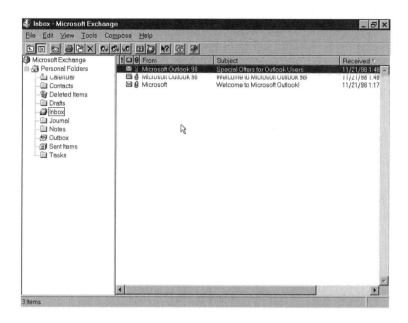

FIGURE 3.10   The Windows NT client.

As in the case of the Windows 3.1x client, support for MS Mail and Windows for Workgroups post offices is provided. This is an excellent feature for helping manage a migration from MS Mail to Exchange.

The minimum requirements for using the Windows NT client are as follows:

- Windows NT 3.51 and higher

- 16MB of RAM

- 12MB of available hard drive space

- Network connection to the Microsoft Exchange 5.5 Server

- Modem

Configuration information for the Exchange Windows NT client is stored in the system Registry.

Different user-specific information can be stored in profiles using the Exchange Windows NT client. This use of profiles makes it possible to configure the Exchange Windows NT client to access email for multiple users on one machine. You can also use profiles to access multiple email services.

MACINTOSH CLIENT

The Macintosh client is a native Macintosh application featuring support for all basic and advanced Exchange features.

To support meeting and appointment requests, the Schedule+ program is installed with the Macintosh client. The Exchange Macintosh client and Schedule+ work in tandem to support the time management features of Exchange.

The following are minimum requirements for using the Macintosh client:

* Macintosh System 7 or higher

* 8MB of RAM

* 14MB of available hard drive space

* Network connection to the Microsoft Exchange 5.5 Server

* Modem

In this lesson you learned about Outlook and the various Exchange clients available. You also learned about system requirements and features. In the next lesson, you will learn how to prepare for the Exchange installation.

Lesson 4

Preparing for a Microsoft Exchange 5.5 Installation

In this lesson you'll learn how to prepare for a Microsoft Exchange 5.5 installation, including the minimum functional system requirements. You'll also learn about the role of the service account and other requirements.

As I've noted in the first chapters, Microsoft Exchange 5.5 is a very advanced product. Microsoft designed Exchange 5.5 to be flexible, while offering as many advanced features as possible.

The Exchange Family Tree

One of the first hurdles in configuring a Microsoft Exchange 5.5 installation is understanding the Microsoft Exchange 5.5 architecture.

Microsoft Exchange 5.5 is organized hierarchically with containers that include configuration objects. If you think of it in the structure of a family you can visualize it easier.

There are three main levels to the Microsoft Exchange 5.5 hierarchy: Organization, Site, and Server. Think of the Organization as the grandparent, the Site as the parent, and the Server as the child, and you'll be set.

Organization—Grandparent Level

The top of the Microsoft Exchange 5.5 hierarchy is the Organization object. This is the grandparent of the organization; all the other objects in the organization are parents or children. :Any configuration changes made at the Organization level apply to the sites and servers in the same family. Because of this top-level design, there is typically only one Organization in each company or installation.

SITE—PARENT LEVEL

The Site object is the parent level. Consisting of one or more Microsoft Exchange 5.5 servers, the Site object creates a transparent location for users. This means a user doesn't need to know the specific Microsoft Exchange 5.5 server to send mail to. The user sees: all users in a site as if they were on one large server. As with Organizations, any changes applied to the Site object are applied to all servers in the site. All servers in a site must be connected via a communication line and must be in the same domain.

SERVERS—CHILD LEVEL

The Server objects are computers running the Microsoft Exchange 5.5 software. Contained within these servers are the individual objects, such as mailboxes, distribution lists, :connectors, and other server-specific information. The server inherits configuration changes from the site, but you can also configure servers individually.

Figure 4.1 shows the relationship among organizations, sites, and servers.

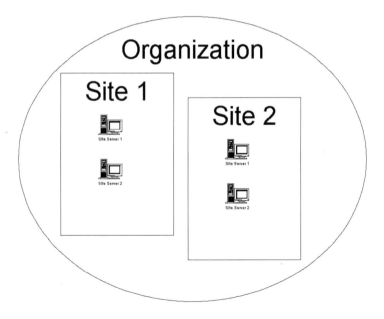

FIGURE 4.1   The relationship among the Organization, Site, and Server objects.

To ensure you maintain flexibility in your Microsoft Exchange 5.5 installation, it's crucial to prepare to do the following:

- Plan the architecture of your Exchange network.
- Select an administrative account for use with Exchange as a service account.
- Ensure your server meets the recommended hardware and software requirements.
- Ensure your server has a solid networking configuration. This includes valid TCP/IP addresses on the proper subnet.
- Determine if you will be connecting to other Exchange sites.
- Determine if you will be connecting to foreign email systems.
- Determine if you will be connecting to the Internet for email connectivity.
- Determine if you will be using Outlook Web Access.
- Document a list of users and distribution lists you want to add to the Exchange server.

The more thorough your pre-planning is, the easier the installation will be.

SERVICE ACCOUNT CREATION

Exchange needs administrator access to ensure that Microsoft Exchange 5.5 works properly. The administrative account you create is called a *service account*.

 Service Account   A service account is a normal Windows NT Server 4.0 user account with special permissions for accessing Microsoft Exchange 5.5. The service account is used for performing behind-the-scene tasks, such as transferring email and performing directory updates.

Exchange uses the service account you create for starting and stopping the Windows NT services that make up the core of Microsoft Exchange 5.5. Figure 4.2 shows the dialog box Exchange presents, requiring you to create the service account.

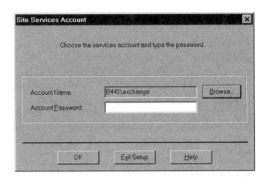

FIGURE 4.2   Exchange requires a service account.

During the installation process, Exchange will ask you for the service account name. You can easily create this account by completing the following steps:

1. From the main menu of the Windows NT server, click on the **Start** menu.

2. Choose **Programs**.

3. Click the **Administrative Tools Common** program group.

4. Run the **User Manager for Domains** by clicking its icon.

5. From the **User** menu, select **New User**.

6. Enter the name for the service account in the **Username** field. A good name to select is **EXCHANGE**.

7. Enter the password for the service account in the **Password** field.

8. Enter the password for the service account in the **Confirm Password** field.

Selecting Features   You enable or disable features by clicking the box to the left of the option. A check mark indicates the option has been enabled.

9. Enable the option **User Cannot Change Password**.

10. Enable the option **Password Never Expires**.

11. Disable the option **User Must Change Password at Next Logon**.

12. Disable the option **Account Disabled** . Your dialog box will now resemble the one in Figure 4.3.

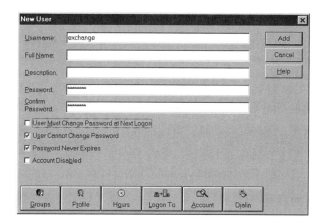

FIGURE **4.3**   Creating the service account.

13. Click the **Add** button.

14. Click the **Close** button.

 Choose a Good Password   Choose a password for the service account. After your Exchange infrastructure is set up, it is quite difficult to change this password successfully if the exchange service account is compromised.

HARDWARE AND SOFTWARE REQUIREMENTS

Microsoft understates Microsoft Exchange 5.5 hardware and software requirements. The minimum requirements according to Microsoft are as follows:

- An Intel Pentium processor of 60MHz or faster.

- 250MB of available hard drive space.

- 64MB of RAM.

- A pagefile of 50MB plus amount of physical RAM. For instance, if your server has 128MB of RAM, your pagefile would be 178MB: 50MB plus 128MB for physical RAM.

- Windows NT Server 4.0 with Service Pack 3.

Exchange *will* function with the minimum requirements, but if you are installing Exchange in an office organization of more than a handful of users, the performance will be far from satisfactory. Instead, you should use the following real-world guidelines:

- An Intel Pentium 233Mhz or faster processor.

- 1 gigabyte of available hard drive space for Microsoft Exchange 5.5 system files, mailboxes, and public folders.

- 128MB of RAM.

- A pagefile of 100MB plus amount of physical RAM. For instance, if your server has 128MB of RAM your pagefile would be 228MB: 100MB plus 128MB for physical RAM.

- Windows NT Server 4.0 with Service Pack 3.

Decide How to Duplicate   A configuration decision you should consider is duplicating disk controllers and drives. You can choose to store the Microsoft Exchange 5.5. transaction logs on a different controller and drive; by doing this you will increase the speed of your Microsoft Exchange 5.5 system.

For a Microsoft Exchange 5.5 installation, the priority of resource availability is memory, processor, and hard drive space, in descending order of importance.

Exchange is a very memory-intensive application. It's important that Exchange has enough available physical memory to handle the user requests as they arrive.

The speed of the processor will be felt most in Exchange's capability to handle background tasks such as directory replication, synchronization, and connector communications.

Hard drive space is important for proper storage of private and public information stores. Without the necessary hard drive space, Exchange might not be able to properly service clients.

MAKE SURE YOUR SERVER IS BUFF ENOUGH

Don't underestimate the resources Microsoft Exchange 5.5 requires. The following guidelines should be followed when trying to ascertain Exchange resource requirements:

- 1–25 users—Accept real-world recommendations

- 26–50 users—Accept real-world recommendations plus 25 percent

- 51–100 users—Accept real-world recommendations plus 50 percent.

- 101–150 users—Accept real-world recommendations plus 75 percent

- 151–200 users—Accept real-world recommendations plus 100 percent.

Installations with over 200 users need to scale requirements in accordance with their heaviest Exchange needs. For example, an organization with 400 users who mainly communicate on the Internet, needs to increase their memory and processor requirements.

NETWORK CONFIGURATION

Microsoft Exchange 5.5 requires a valid network configuration. This connection includes ensuring an adapter card is installed and functioning, as well as verifying that TCP/IP is activated with valid addresses.

You can verify the network configuration by completing the following steps:

1. From the main Windows NT Server screen, click the **Start** menu.

2. Choose **Settings**.

3. Choose **Control Panel**.

4. When the Control Panel opens, double-click the **Network** icon.

5. Select the **Adapters** tab and verify the proper network interface card driver is loaded.

6. Select the **Protocols** tab and verify the TCP/IP address.

Exchange relies heavily on the TCP/IP protocol to communicate with clients. Using the Remote Procedure Call (RPC) protocol, which runs over TCP/IP, Exchange ensures information transfers between the server and client reliably. You can verify your TCP/IP settings by performing the following steps:

1. Select the **Start** menu.

2. Choose the **Programs** group.

3. Click the **Command Prompt** icon to enter the command-based console of Windows NT, as shown in Figure 4.4.

4. You can access the TCP/IP information by typing **IPCONFIG** at the command prompt. You will be shown a screen with the TCP/IP information, which is similar to Figure 4.5.

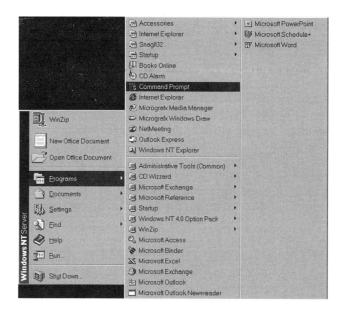

FIGURE **4.4**   Opening a Windows NT 4.0 command prompt.

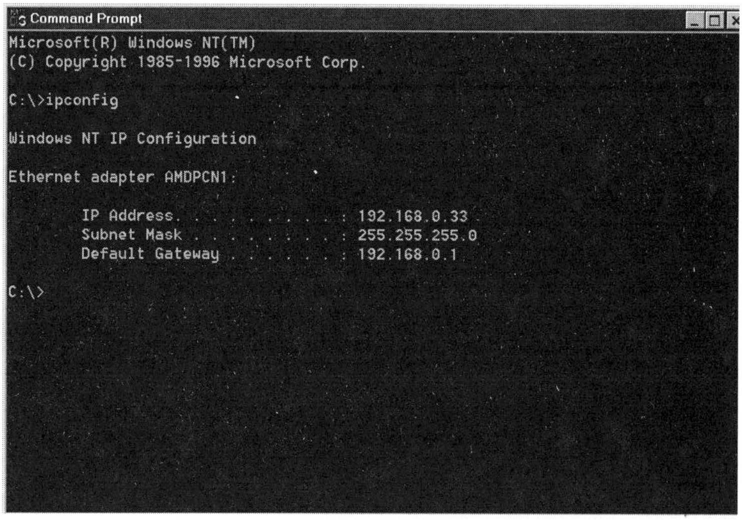

FIGURE **4.5**   Using IPCONFIG to verify Windows NT 4.0 settings.

You should see your TCP/IP address, subnet mask, and default gateway. If you don't see this information you might have to install the TCP/IP protocol. Reinstalling the TCP/IP protocol is covered in Lesson 15, "Client Troubleshooting Guide."

Before you reinstall the TCP/IP protocol, check the cable connection to the client. Ensure that the cable is secure in the socket of the NIC with a link light (if one is available).

Although Exchange works in conjunction with protocols other than TCP/IP with RPC, using it with those two protocols is the standard configuration. To use other protocols for communication between the server and clients, you need to add the protocol onto each of the client machines.

 Check RFC Filtering   Some of the older switches and intelligent hubs sometimes filtered RPC traffic. If you have issues connecting to your Exchange server, verify that your infrastructure is not filtering RPC.

CONNECTING TO FOREIGN EMAIL SYSTEMS

Microsoft Exchange 5.5 provides native support for connecting to other email systems. Microsoft Exchange 5.5 can exchange mail with the following systems:

- cc:Mail from Lotus
- MS Mail from Microsoft
- X.400
- AppleTalk Networks—Quarterdeck Mail

CONNECTING TO THE WORLD

Email uses *connectors* to get from your Exchange server to different types of email systems.

Connectors   Connectors are the bridges used to connect one email system to another. They can either connect Microsoft Exchange Servers to another Microsoft Exchange Server or to a foreign email system.

Connectors are software modules written by Microsoft to perform the single task of translating email from Exchange to a foreign email system. For example, you might hear the term *cc:Mail connector*. This refers to how the software module processes an Exchange message into a cc:Mail message, and then submits the message for delivery to the Mail Transfer Agent (MTA).

A simple way to conceptualize connectors is to think of a three-prong adapter plug for your house. In older homes the electrical outlets only feature two prongs. If you want to plug in a three-prong device, such as your computer, you need an adapter. The adapter converts the plug from three prongs to two prongs so you can plug it in.

This is exactly what a connector does. It takes an Exchange formatted message and converts it to the foreign email system's format.

Before installing Exchange, ensure you have the following information for each foreign email system:

- **Administrator ID and password for the foreign email account**—Typically, you'll need this information to configure the MTA. The MTA is responsible for transferring mail from one email system to another.

- **Connectivity method**—Will you be connecting to the foreign email system through a dial-up connection or a direct connection?

- **Email administrator contact information**—Ensure you have the name, number, and beeper number of the administrator of the foreign email system. This information allows you to contact them if you encounter any difficulties setting up your connector to their system.

Each of the foreign email connectors has a different installation routine; these are covered in Lesson 10, "Connecting Microsoft Exchange 5.5 with MS Mail for PC Networks."

CONNECTING TO THE INTERNET

Microsoft Exchange 5.5 has developed their Internet email connectivity to a point where it is a very powerful component. Exchange's Internet connectivity package is called, appropriately enough, the Internet Mail Service, and is shown in Figure 4.6.

FIGURE 4.6   Exchange's Internet Mail Service.

The Internet Mail Service relies on the following three standard Internet components to route your email messages through the Internet:

- **SMTP**—Simple Mail Transfer Protocol is used for sending mail from one post office to another. Exchange uses this protocol to send email from your server to another SMTP capable server on the Internet. SMTP is used on a wide variety of email servers, including Microsoft Exchange, UNIX, NetWare, and Linux.

- **TCP/IP**—Transmission Control Protocol/Internet Protocol manages the actual communication portion of the mail transfer. Think of TCP/IP as the rules to navigate the Internet.

- **DNS**—The Domain Name System is used to look up domain name addresses and convert them to their TCP/IP counterparts. The DNS takes the domain name of the company you are trying to send a message to, for instance COMPUNOTES.COM, and resolves the actual TCP/IP address, 209.100.53.43. The domain name can be thought of as someone's last name, whereas the TCP/IP address is their street, city, state, and ZIP code.

You need to note if you will be connecting to the Internet before you install Exchange. The IMS is an optional component of the Exchange installation process. For an easy configuration, you should include it at the same time you install Exchange.

YOUR INTERNET SERVICE PROVIDER (ISP)

If you will be sending email through the Internet, you need an Internet service provider (ISP). An ISP provides access the Internet.

You can connect to the Internet using either a dial-up connection through Windows NT Server Remote Access Service (RAS) or a dedicated connection such as frame relay, T1 or ISDN.

There are two pieces of information you need from your ISP before you can connect your Exchange server to the Internet:

- **DNS TCP/IP address**—If your company doesn't have a DNS server, you'll need to ensure you use your ISP's DNS server for email routing.

- **Assigned TCP/IP address subnet**—If your company doesn't have a registered TCP/IP address, you'll need to secure at least one for your connection to the ISP. The router you choose should have security features built-in to prevent casual access to your system from the Internet.

OUTLOOK WEB ACCESS

One of the more exciting features of Microsoft Exchange 5.5 is that it offers clients the ability to check their email with an Internet connection through Outlook Web Access.

Outlook Web Access provides an HTML front end to a simple Outlook client, shown in Figure 4.7. From this front end, any user whose browser supports JavaScript and frames can send and receive email, access their folders, and access public folders.

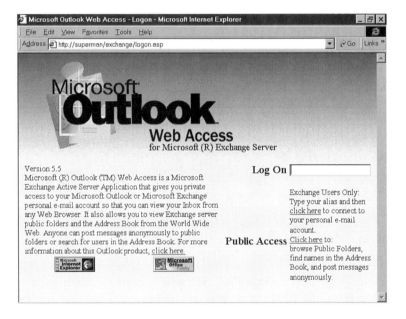

FIGURE 4.7   Outlook Web Access.

To harness the power of this feature, you need to ensure that Internet Information Server (IIS) is installed on your Windows NT Server. IIS supplies the Web server interface needed to provide access to Internet clients.

 Use The Right IIS Version   You need IIS 3.0 or above. The standard IIS version is 2.0, which accompanies a new installation of Windows NT Server 4.0 . IIS version 2.0 doesn't support active server pages, but you can upgrade to IIS version 3.0 by installing Windows NT Server Service Pack 3.0 or higher, or by downloading the Windows NT Server Option pack.

You'll need to determine the *authentication method* you want to use when you install Outlook Web Access. The authentication method relates to the security features for users when they enter their logon information. You can choose from the following three authentication methods:

- **Basic authentication**—The lowest level of authentication, this is a good choice if all the users are on an intranet. You do not want to select this method if you are offering connectivity from the Internet. All browsers support this type of encryption.

- **Windows NT Challenge/Response authentication**—Using Microsoft's own authentication method, this is a good choice if you are offer intranet and Internet access. The main limitation is that your IIS installation needs to be on the same server as your Exchange installation. In a large organization, this might not be possible.

- **Secure Sockets Layer authentication**—The most secure authentication option available; Secure Sockets Layer (SSL) offers complete encryption. This is the best choice if you offer access from the Internet. Not all browsers completely support SSL, but the newer generation of browsers from Netscape and Microsoft do.

Outlook Web Access Is Versatile   Outlook Web Access not only supports your Windows 3.1x, Windows 95/98, and Windows NT clients, but it also supports any computer that has a Java-enabled browser with frames support. This means you can offer email to your UNIX, Macintosh, and other clients whose browsers support Java and frames.

Outlook Web Access is a solid tool for offering your remote or mobile users email access. You need to pay attention to the security risks and issues; as long as you protect yourself adequately up front, your back end will be protected.

User and Distribution List Preparation

After you've completed your Microsoft Exchange 5.5 installation, you'll be ready to test and use it. You can't do that unless you have users added to the system. An Exchange server without users is like a sports car without an engine. Sure, it looks nice, but you can't do anything with it.

Naming Conventions

The first decision you'll have to make concerning users and distribution lists is the *naming convention*. A naming convention is a formula to determine a user's ID under Exchange Server.

There are several methods of naming conventions that work. Use Table 4.1 to help you decide.

TABLE 4.1 EXCHANGE NAMING CONVENTION OPTIONS

CONVENTION	EXAMPLE	DUPLICATES
First initial of first name followed by last name.	The user Patrick Grote would become PGROTE.	Duplicates would be handled by adding the second letter of the first name to the user ID. Patrick Grote would become PAGROTE.
First name followed by last initial.	The user Patrick Grote would become PATRICKG.	Duplicates would be handled by adding the second letter of the last name to the user ID. Patrick Grote would become PATRICKGR.

CONVENTION	EXAMPLE	DUPLICATES
Employee ID Number.	If Patrick Grote's user ID were 343-68-1968 the user ID would become 343681968.	There would be no duplicate IDs
Department Number and Name.	Patrick Grote is in the IT department, which has a number of 68. His ID would be 68PGROTE.	Duplicates would be handled by adding the second letter of the first name to the user ID. Patrick Grote in the IT department would become 68PAGROTE.

TABLE 4.2 EXCHANGE NAMING CONVENTION OPTIONS

CONVENTION	BENEFITS	ISSUES
First initial of first name followed by last name.	Easy to reconcile user ID to username. Good for large organizations.	For large organizations the directory might be with multiple IDs that look alike.
First name followed by last initial.	More casual and easier to understand for small groups.	Greater potential for duplicate IDs.
Employee ID Number.	Guaranteed unique address.	Cold andThere unintuitive name would be difficult to reconcile.
Department Number and Name.	Makes navigating and reconciling addresses easier.	Department numbers might change. New users do not know department numbers.

INVENTORY OF USER NAMES AND DISTRIBUTION LISTS

The next step is to ensure you have a complete list of usernames to add to the system. Remember to follow the naming conventions so you can pre-determine the number of duplicates.

Distribution lists are groups of users, called members, with a common theme. When an email message is sent to the distribution list, all members of the list receive a copy. For example, a distribution list is named ALLUSERS and each Exchange ID is added to it. If you check the properties of ALLUSERS, it shows every user in the organization. A message sent to ALLUSERS delivers the message to every user in the organization, but you only have to add a single address.

 Distribution Lists   Logical groupings of users to help ease mailing of messages. Each user in a distribution list is called a *member*. When a message is sent to a distribution list, each of the members receives a copy. For instance, you might want to create a distribution list for all employees. When you need to send a message to every employee, all you have to do is select the ALLUSERS distribution list, and each member of the list will receive a copy of your message.

Exchange supports global distribution lists and personal distribution lists. *Global distribution* lists are available for use by everyone through the Global Address List (GAL), and personal distribution lists are available only to the user who created them.

In this lesson, you learned what is needed to prepare for a Microsoft Exchange 5.5 installation. You verified your system has met the minimum functional system requirements and created a service account. You also learned about the Microsoft Exchange 5.5 infrastructure. In the next lesson, you'll begin the actual installation process.

Lesson 5

Installing Microsoft Exchange

In this lesson, you'll conquer the installation of Microsoft Exchange 5.5.

Installing Microsoft Exchange 5.5 is similar to installing other Microsoft products. You just need to follow the onscreen prompts and enter the requested information.

Take your time during installation and follow along with these instructions:

1. Place your Microsoft Exchange 5.5 CD-ROM into the CD-ROM drive of the server on which you would like to install Microsoft Exchange 5.5.

2. If you have Autoplay enabled on your server, you will see the introduction screen for Microsoft Exchange 5.5 shown in Figure 5.1.

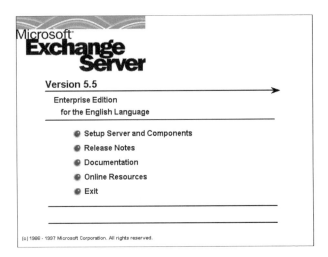

FIGURE 5.1   The Microsoft Exchange 5.5 introduction screen.

3. Click on **Setup Server and Components**.

4. In the options screen shown in Figure 5.2, click on **Microsoft Exchange Server 5.5**. You will notice the installation routine copies several setup files to your hard drive. You're then presented with the opening installation routine described in step 6; so skip ahead to that section.

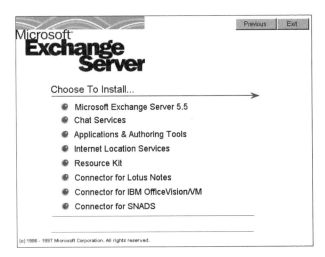

FIGURE 5.2   Select Microsoft Exchange 5.5.

5. If you don't have Autoplay enabled, click the **Start** menu, choose **Run**, and then type **D:\SERVER\SETUP\I386\Setup.exe** (where **D:** is the drive letter of your CD-ROM). You're then presented with the license agreement dialog box shown in Figure 5.3.

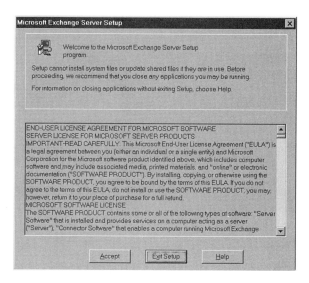

FIGURE **5.3**   The License Agreement screen.

6. Click **Accept**. You'll then be presented with the Exchange Server Setup dialog box shown in Figure 5.4. If you have Autoplay enabled, this is where you come in.

FIGURE 5.4   The Exchange Server Setup screen.

7. Select the **Complete/Custom** option. You'll then be presented with the choices for installation shown in Figure 5.5.

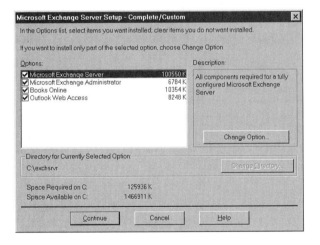

FIGURE 5.5   Selecting Complete/Custom.

8. Select **Continue**. At this point, if you do not have Active Server Pages for Internet Information Server (IIS) installed, you will receive the warning shown in Figure 5.6.

FIGURE 5.6   The Active Server Page warning.

9. If IIS is currently running, the Exchange installation routine will
    stop the IIS services and you'll see the dialog box shown in
    Figure 5.7.

FIGURE 5.7   Stopping the IIS services.

10. You are now the presented with the CD Key dialog box shown in
    Figure 5.8. Enter the CD Key located on the back of your CD
    jewel case.

 Protect the CD Key   It's a good idea to make a copy
of the CD Key number and put it in a safe place just in
case something happens to the jewel case.

FIGURE 5.8   Enter your CD Key Information here.

11. Click on **OK** when you are prompted to verify the CD Key. You will then be presented with the Organization and Site configuration screen shown in Figure 5.9.

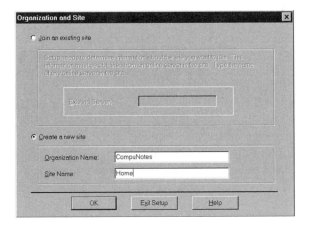

FIGURE 5.9   Organization and Site information.

12. Because this is a new installation, you need to enter the organization and site name. Think of your organization as your business name. The site name should correspond to the location, function, or number of Exchange Servers being installed. Some examples of organization and site names: **MAIN/SERVER1,**

BIGCOMPANY/TEXAS, WPGLTD/ACCOUNTING or **TECHCO/FLOOR2.** After you enter the organization and site information select **OK** and then verify your entries by clicking Yes. You are then presented with the Site Services Account dialog box, as shown in Figure 5.10.

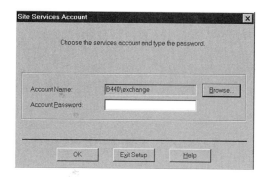

FIGURE 5.10   The Site Services Account.

13. In your pre-planning in Lesson 4, "Preparing for a Microsoft Exchange 5.5 Installation," you created the Exchange Services Account. Our example account was **EXCHANGE.** Enter the account name and password and then select **OK.** Exchange grants certain rights to the Services Account before continuing the installation; it presents the dialog box shown in Figure 5.11 for confirmation. Click on **OK** to continue.

FIGURE 5.11   Site Services Attributes.

14. Exchange then verifies that your system is ready for installation. You will see the dialog box shown in Figure 5.12 as this happens.

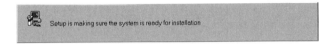

FIGURE 5.12   Verifying system readiness.

15. As soon as the Exchange installation routine determines your server can handle Exchange, the installation routine begins copying files. You'll see the progress dialog box shown in Figure 5.13.

FIGURE 5.13   Copying Exchange files.

16. When the files are finished copying, Exchange begins installing the services and modifying the Registry, presenting the dialog box shown in Figure 5.14. You'll notice that all the Exchange services will start and Outlook Web Access is installed.

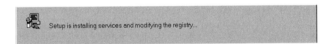

FIGURE 5.14   Starting services and modifying the Registry.

17. After the copy process is complete, you can either end the installation or run Exchange Server Optimizer, as shown in Figure 5.15. At this point you should run the Optimizer; click **Run Optimizer**. Exchange Server Optimizer examines your system resources and Exchange configuration, and then optimizes your system for maximum performance.

FIGURE 5.15   Running the Exchange Server Optimizer.

18. The main Exchange Server Optimizer Wizard warns you it needs
    to shut down Exchange services, as shown in Figure 5.16. Click
    Next.

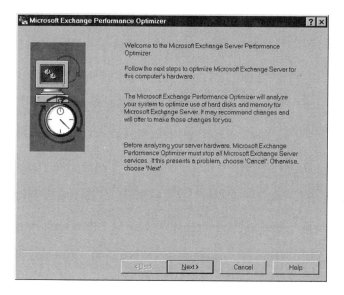

FIGURE 5.16   Stopping Exchange services.

19. When the services have been stopped, you will be presented
    with a configuration dialog box for Exchange Performance
    Optimizer, as shown in Figure 5.17. The goal of this screen is to
    ensure Exchange is optimized to your organization or goals for

the Exchange Server. Select the information that is appropriate
to your installation and click **Next**. You will then be asked to
confirm your settings. Click **Next** to continue.

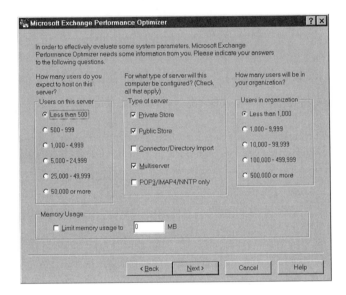

FIGURE 5.17   Configuring Exchange Performance Optimizer.

The following describes the available options for Exchange
Server Optimizer:

- **Users on This Server**—This field should contain the number of Microsoft Exchange 5.5 users you expect on this
  server. Estimate for growth by adding 10 percent.

- **Type of Server**—You should select the attributes that best
  describe your server.

- **Private Store**—Will you have private mail messages and
  other personal files?

- **Public Store**—Will you have public folders and other
  public files?

- **Connector/Directory Import**—Will this server be connecting to a foreign email system?

- **Multiserver**—Is there more than one server in this site?

- **POP3/IMAP4/NNTP Only**—Will you use this server for Internet clients only?

- **Users in Organization**—This field should contain the number of users your expect in the entire organization. Keep in mind this includes all the sites.

- **Memory Usage**—If you are running IIS, SQL Server, or another BackOffice product on this server you might want to limit the amount of memory Microsoft Exchange 5.5 uses.

20. Taking your configuration information and the system configuration, Exchange Server Optimizer begins working, presenting the progress dialog box shown in Figure 5.18. After it is finished, the Exchange Server Optimizer restarts the necessary Exchange services.

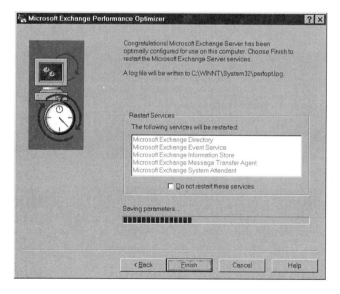

FIGURE **5.18**   The Exchange Server Optimizer in progress.

CONGRATULATIONS

You have now accomplished something mystical and magical! Your Microsoft Exchange 5.5 server is ready to perform. In this lesson, you've installed and configured Exchange Server, specifying the appropriate options for your organization.

In this lesson, you've taken your first step in harnessing the power of Microsoft Exchange 5.5 by installing the server software. In the next lesson, you'll work to configure your installation.

Lesson 6

Configuring Microsoft Exchange 5.5

In this lesson, you'll learn how to configure Microsoft Exchange 5.5 for your installation. You'll also be looking closely at the Exchange Administrator program.

Have you ever been so excited about anticipating something that when you finally get it, you feel overwhelmed? That's quite possibly how you are feeling right now. You have this workhorse Microsoft Exchange 5.5 installed—a significant accomplishment—but now you have to configure it for your business.

Your Command Arsenal

Before you become intimidated and question your ability to control Exchange, listen to this good news: Microsoft supplies you with the necessary tool to tame Exchange—the *Exchange Administrator*.

The Exchange Administrator software is a native Windows NT program designed to manage your Exchange installation. By using the Exchange Administrator, you'll be able to accomplish the following tasks and more:

- Create, delete, and modify user accounts
- Create, delete, and modify site information
- Configure the Exchange services
- Configure the connectors
- Configure the Mail Transfer Agent (MTA)
- Configure and modify protocols

Exchange automatically installs all the tools you need to configure your Exchange installation. Click the **Start menu**, choose **Programs**, and select **Microsoft Exchange**, and you will see all the utilities that have been installed, as shown in Figure 6.1.

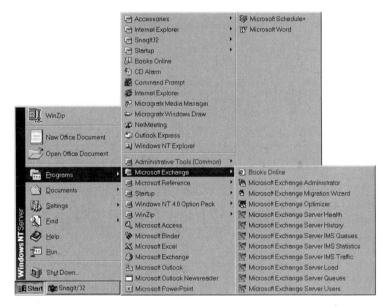

Figure **6.1**   The Exchange Utility programs.

Don't panic! Not all these choices are actually programs. Most of them load Performance Monitor with default settings to help you monitor your Exchange performance. You'll cover more on performance in Lesson 16, "Microsoft Exchange Server 5.5 Server Troubleshooting".

THE EXCHANGE ADMINISTRATOR

To start the Exchange Administrator click the **Start menu**, choose **Programs**, click **Microsoft Exchange**, and select **Microsoft Exchange Administrator**. You will then be prompted to enter a server name, as shown in Figure 6.2.

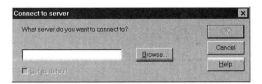

FIGURE 6.2   Entering a server name.

For the server name, enter the local machine that you installed onto.
You'll then see the Exchange Administrator program window, as shown in
Figure 6.3. The first thing you'll notice is that the interface looks familiar.
Yes, it looks very similar to Windows Explorer. However, instead of files
and directories, the Exchange Administrator program displays objects.
There are three main sections to the Exchange Administrator program.

The top section of the program window is the command section, consisting of the menu bar and toolbar. From here, you can control various command aspects of the program such as views, windows, and so on.

The left section of the program window shows the Exchange hierarchy.
The Exchange hierarchy is represented as objects. The high-level objects
are first displayed:

- Organization
- Address Book Views
- Folders
- Global Address List
- Site
- Configuration
- Add-Ins
- Addressing

- Connections
- Directory Replication
- Monitors
- Protocols
- Servers
- Distribution Lists
- Recipients

The right section lists the configuration information for each object. You
can see sample configuration information listed in Figure 6.3.

Organization   Site   Menu bar   Toolbar

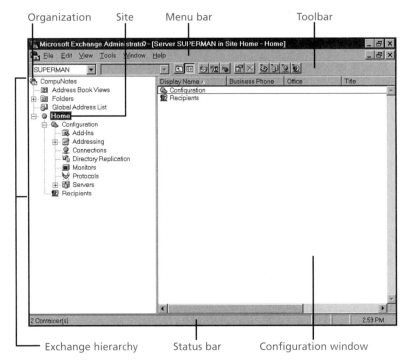

FIGURE 6.3   The sections of the Exchange Administrator.

OBJECTS OF EXCHANGE'S AFFECTION

Objects are Exchange's method of dealing with resources. Each object relates to a specific Exchange resource. By giving the administrator control of each object, the Exchange Administrator becomes a very powerful tool.

So, what do the objects represent? The following section describes each object and its resource. Don't feel as if you need to memorize each object and its function. Your goal should be to familiarize yourself with the object metaphor, and you can always refer back to this lesson if you get stuck.

Organization. The Organization object is the top dog of the Exchange hierarchy. It is referred to as the Container object, because both objects are inside the Organization object. Think of the Organization object as your company. The other objects in the Exchange hierarchy are what you would normally find in a company: desks, employees, computers, and so on. The organization name you entered during installation becomes the object name.

Folders. The Folder object is the container object for public folders and system folders.

The Public Folders object details the configuration information for the organization's public folders. Changes made to this object can be replicated to other Microsoft Exchange 5.5 Servers.

The System Folders object contains the Eforms Registry, Offline Address Book and Schedule+ Free Busy objects.

The Eforms Registry object contains a list of all electronic forms.

The Offline Address Book contains the list of recipient names that can be sent mail by offline users. This object might contain multiple offline address books. Remote users issue a command to download the offline address book.

The Schedule+ Free/Busy object contains the scheduling information for users who use Schedule+. When a user is sent a request for a meeting or creates a meeting request, this object is updated to reflect the new information.

Global Address List. The Global Address List object displays all the mailboxes, distribution lists, public folders, and custom recipients in your organization. Any object that can be a *recipient* (have a message sent to it) will appear here.

Site. The Site object contains the Configuration and Recipients' objects. As an Exchange administrator, a majority of your changes to the Exchange server will happen here. The site you entered during installation becomes the object name.

Configuration. The Configuration object is the container for site-specific configuration objects.

Add-Ins. The Add-Ins object contains non-recipient add-ins to the Exchange environment.

Addressing. The Addressing object is a container for the Details template, the Email Address Generator, and the One-Off Address templates.

The Details Template object contains recipient language and country settings.

The Email Address Generator object contains the email address generators. Exchange uses DLL files to generate email addresses. You can find the cc:Mail, Internet, Microsoft Exchange 5.5 Mail, and X.400 generators in this object.

The *One-Off Address templates* are templates that you use to address messages to mailboxes that are not in your Global Address List or in your personal address book.

 One-Off Address Templates These templates are so named because they are often used to send *one* piece of mail *off* to an address and are not used again.

Connections. The Connections object is a container for the Connector object. A *connector* is used to tie an Exchange site with another email system. The other email system can be another Exchange site, the Internet, or a foreign email system. The connectors supplied with Microsoft Exchange 5.5 that you might see include

- **Site Connector**—Responsible for connecting one Exchange site to another

- **X.400 Connector**—Responsible for connecting Microsoft Exchange 5.5 sites over an X.400 network

- **Dynamic RAS Connector**—Responsible for connecting Microsoft Exchange 5.5 sites over an RAS connection

- **Microsoft Mail Connector**—Responsible for connecting Microsoft Exchange 5.5 sites to an MS Mail post office

- **Internet Mail Service**—Responsible for transferring messages from the Microsoft Exchange 5.5 site to the Internet using SMTP

- **cc:Mail Connector**—Responsible for connecting the Microsoft Exchange 5.5 site to a cc:Mail installation

- **Microsoft Mail Connector for AppleTalk Networks**— Responsible for connecting the Microsoft Exchange 5.5 site to AppleTalk networks

- **Directory Exchange Server**—Responsible for performing directory synchronization with other messaging systems

- **Directory Exchange Requestor**—Responsible for requesting directory information from other message systems

- **DirSync Server**—Responsible for processing updates from the Directory Exchange Requestor as custom recipients

- **Remote DirSync Requestor**—Responsible for responding to requests from foreign email systems concerning address and directory authentication

Directory Replication. The Directory Replication object is a container for all directory replication connectors. A directory replication is used to share information among sites.

Monitors. The Monitors object contains the utilities that monitor the health of the Exchange server and the associated links.

Protocols. The Protocols object is the container for all Internet-related protocols. Included in this container are the following objects:

- **HTTP**—Hypertext Transfer Protocol allows users to access their email box through the Internet when using Outlook Web Access.

- **IMAP4**—Internet Message Access Protocol, version 4, allows users to access their Exchange mailbox as well as, private and public folders.

- **LDAP**—Lightweight Directory Access Protocol allows users with LDAP-compatible email programs to search and read directories. Security is available when using LDAP.

- **NNTP**—Network News Transfer Protocol is used to bring Internet newsgroup support to Microsoft Exchange 5.5.

- **POP3**—Post Office Protocol 3 allows users to read and send email using their Exchange mailbox from any POP3-compatible email client.

Servers. The Server object is a container for server-specific configuration settings within a site. If you have multiple servers, you will see each listed here by name. Included within this container are the following objects:

- **Private Information Store**—The Private Information Store object stores all the messages sent to mailboxes. It is also in the container object for the following two resources:

  - **Logons**—The Logons object allows you to view information about the Logon history of each user.

  - **Mailbox Resources**—The Mailbox Resources object allows you to view how much space each mailbox occupies and how many items they contain.

- **Protocols**—The Protocols object is the container for all Internet-related protocols. This is the same information contained in the Configuration and Protocols objects mentioned earlier.

- **Public Information Store**—The Public Information Store contains all the public messages for a server. It also serves as the container for the Folder Replication Status, Logons, Public Folder Resources and Server Replication Status objects.

- **Server Recipients**—The Recipient object contains all the Server specific recipient information.

Recipients. The Recipients object contains all the site-specific recipient information.

AN OBJECT LESSON •

As you work with objects, you will start to understand that there are site-specific objects and server-specific objects.

Site-specific objects contain all the server-specific objects. For example, if site A contains Servers B, C and D, Site A's objects would include Servers B, C and D's objects, as shown in Figure 6.4. If you looked at Server A's objects, though, It would not Include Server B or Server C objects.

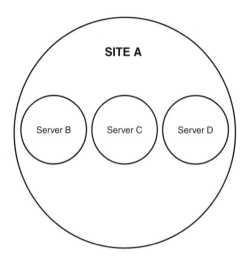

FIGURE 6.4   Site versus Server objects.

PUTTING EXCHANGE ADMINISTRATOR TO WORK

Getting into the meat of the Exchange Administrator is best accomplished by using the menu commands. As you become more familiar with the menu commands, you can move to the command toolbar. There are six choices on the menu bar: **File**, **Edit**, **View**, **Tools**, **Window**, and **Help**. It's pretty standard.

As you will see, each of the menu commands contain options that only become available when certain objects are selected. A non-functioning command will be grayed out, whereas available commands will appear as normal text.

THE FILE MENU

The File menu, shown in Figure 6.5, is used to connect to Exchange servers, create and modify objects, and view object properties, among other things.

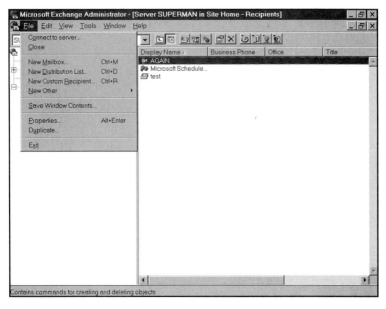

FIGURE 6.5   The Exchange Administrator File commands.

The available commands are as follows:

Connect to Server. This command allows you to open a server for administration. When you choose this command, you'll see the dialog box in Figure 6.6. You can type the name of the server you'd like to connect to or use the **Browse** command. After the server is selected, the Exchange Administrator opens to the main menu where you see the object hierarchy.

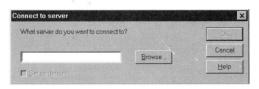

FIGURE 6.6   The Exchange Administrator Connect to Server command.

The Exchange Administrator uses a Multiple Document Interface (MDI), in which you can open multiple servers to work on. As noted in Figure 6.7, you can even tile the window views to maximize your administration effort. To do so, choose **Tile Horizontally** or **Tile Vertically** from the **Window** menu.

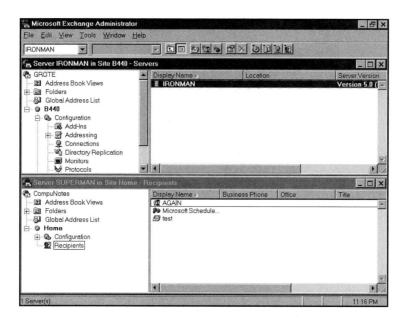

FIGURE 6.7   The Exchange Administrator Multiple Server interface.

Pick the Right Server   When working with multiple servers you should be careful that the changes you are making are on the server you want. From time to time, you might be confused about which server you are working on. You can always look to the header and verify the server before you affect the change.

Leave a Window Open   Microsoft Exchange remembers the windows you had open last time the Exchange Administrator was running and opens them again when you launch the program.

Close. Close simply closes the current server you are administrating. If no servers are open, the Close command is unavailable.

New Mailbox. The New Mailbox command is probably the command you will use the most when creating your Microsoft Exchange Server 5.5. New mailboxes can only be created in the recipient container. If you aren't in a recipient container, Exchange Administrator will prompt you to move to it.

As shown in Figure 6.8, you can specify multiple configuration properties when you create a mailbox. You will examine these attributes in detail in Lesson 11, "Managing Users".

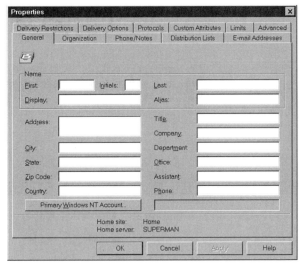

FIGURE 6.8   The Exchange Administrator New Mailbox command.

New Distribution List. The New Distribution List command is, not surprisingly, responsible for creating distribution lists. Distribution lists need to be created in the recipients container.

As you can see in Figure 6.9, there are many options for distribution lists. You'll cover these options in Lesson 11.

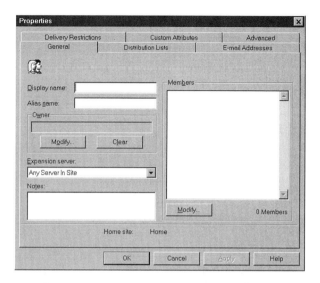

FIGURE 6.9   The Exchange Administrator New Distribution List
command results in this dialog box.

New Custom Recipient. The New Custom Recipient command is used to
create recipient objects located on foreign email systems. You might use
this option for an Internet address, cc:Mail address, or other foreign email
system.

As you can see in Figure 6.10, connectors you have installed represent the
available email systems. There is a unique Other Addresses option that
allows you to add non-connector addresses.

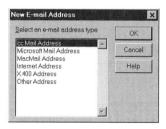

FIGURE 6.10   The Exchange Administrator New Custom Recipient
command produces this dialog box.

Uses for Custom Recipients Custom recipients are great for adding secondary Internet email addresses or pagers. Some users today are even adding their digital phones as custom recipients.

New Other. This is a command you won't necessarily use to install and configure your Microsoft Exchange 5.5 installation. The objects created using New Other are typically more advanced. Figure 6.11 shows the objects that can be created.

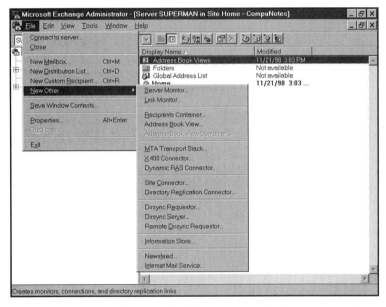

FIGURE **6.11**   The Exchange Administrator New Other command.

Save Windows Contents. This is one of the neater commands created by Microsoft. It allows you to save the contents of the active windows to a comma-delimited file, and is great for getting a quick dump of user or distribution objects.

Properties. This command shows you the properties of a specific object. For instance, clicking Properties on a user will display the properties for that user. Typically, you can double-click on an object to view the properties, but you might find it necessary to use this menu command.

Duplicate. The Duplicate command creates a duplicate object of the object that is highlighted. If you were to duplicate a user, it would create a user with no name, but with the attributes of the duplicated user. This is a great time-saving feature when you need to populate an Exchange server quickly.

Exit. This command, of course, shuts down the Exchange Administrator program.

THE EDIT MENU

One of the great features of Exchange Administrator is that it uses standard Windows conventions. This is most evident in the Edit menu. As you can see in Figure 6.12, the standard Windows Edit commands are available: **Undo**, **Cut**, **Copy**, **Paste**, **Delete**, and **Select All**.

FIGURE 6.12   Exchange Administrator Edit menu.

Undo. Don't get too excited about the capability to erase mistakes! The Undo command, as well as the **Cut** and **Paste** commands, only work in text boxes under Exchange. If you make a mistake while editing text, you can undo it using this command.

 Watch Your Commands!—The Undo command won't undo any action performed on an object. It is strictly for text editing. If you delete the president of your company from the recipients container, the Undo command won't help save your job. You need to rebuild the user account.

Cut. This command cuts text from a text box and places it in the Windows Clipboard.

Paste. This command pastes information from the Windows Clipboard into the current text box.

Delete. This command deletes the selected object so be careful, as there is no undo function for it. You should *always* verify the server or site you are deleting objects or containers from.

Select All. This command selects all the objects in the current window view. You can also accomplish this by using the standard windows convention of highlighting the first object, holding down the **Shift** key, and then clicking on the last object.

THE VIEW MENU

Your organization might grow, which means your Exchange server must grow with it. If your server supports many users, it is sometimes easier to *filter* or sort the information you are viewing. You might also want to remove an extra tool or status bar, so you can fit as much information as possible onscreen.

The View menu is your key to making this happen. As you can see in Figure 6.13, there are many choices.

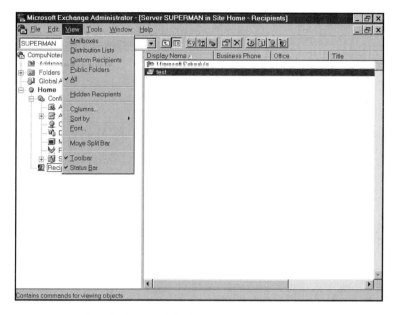

FIGURE 6.13   The Exchange Administrator View menu.

The first five options pertain to *filtering*. Filtering allows you to view only certain types of objects while temporarily hiding the other objects from view. The filter choices are **Mailboxes, Distribution Lists, Custom Recipients, Public Folders**, and **All**.

If you are in a hurry to modify a distribution list for your boss, for example, you could enable the appropriate filter by selecting **View, Distribution Lists**. Exchange Administrator would only show distribution lists. To remove the filter, select **View, All**.

The following commands each control a different aspect of the displayed data:

Hidden Recipients. This command shows all the recipient objects. Certain Recipient objects, such as Internet newsgroups, are hidden. You can use this command to ensure you see even these groups.

A Use for Hidden Recipients   Hidden recipients are a good idea for conducting surveys in your company. The answers could be sent to a hidden recipient. This has two advantages: security, because the recipient object doesn't display anywhere, and hiding the recipient from the Global Address List, because there are certain addresses, such as human resources or accounting, that you might not want to publish. By hiding the recipient, you prevent the address from being published in the Global Address List.

Columns. This is another neat command; it allows you to modify the data fields displayed in the Object view of Exchange Administrator.

Some organizations might want to display a user's custom attributes, modification date, or phone number. Using the **Columns** command, as illustrated in Figure 6.14, you have complete control to display the information that is important to you.

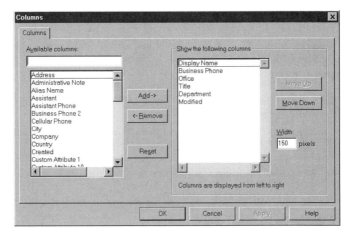

FIGURE 6.14   The Exchange Administrator Columns command.

Sort by. This command is kind of a disappointment. You are limited to sorting by last name or modified date. However, by using the latter option, this command can help you quickly scan and recognize which account records have changed.

Font. This command allows you to select a font to use when viewing the Exchange Administrator.

As you can see in Figure 6.15, the Font dialog box is standard and allows you to select font, style, and size.

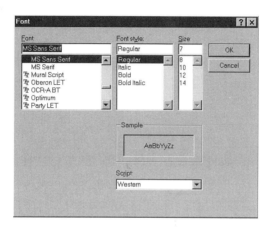

FIGURE 6.15   The Exchange Administrator Font command.

Move Split Bar. This command allows you to move the line separating the left side of the Exchange Administrator from the right. You could typically do this with a mouse, but this command gives you added accessibility.

Toolbar. This command allows you to remove the toolbar from the top of the screen. To redisplay the toolbar, select the Toolbar command again.

Status Bar. This command allows you to remove the status bar from the bottom of the screen. To redisplay the status bar, select the **Status Bar** command again.

 Need More Space?   Removing the toolbar and status bar will give you more screen space. For organizations with a large number of objects, this might be a good idea.

THE TOOLS MENU

The Tools menu, as show in Figure 6.16, contains the majority of admin-istrative-related functions. Although most of these functions are not related to the day-to-day maintenance of an MS installation.

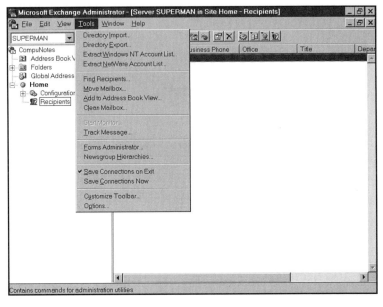

FIGURE 6.16   The Exchange Administrator Tools menu.

You should pay close attention while reading the following descriptions. Your organization might have a need for a certain function that you didn't realize exists until now.

Directory Import. Any opportunity you have to save time and effort when completing an Exchange installation should be seized. Microsoft has added this super function that allows you to import recipients from a comma-delimited file. This is great for creating new recipients or modify-ing existing ones.

As you can see in Figure 6.17, you have complete control over which domain and Exchange Server you can import into. Selecting which recipi-ent container to import into is very important. You can also specify an existing recipient to use as a template or modify existing users. For instance, you can add a standard Custom Attribute field to each user without having to modify each recipient manually.

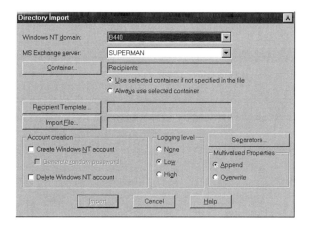

FIGURE 6.17   The Exchange Administrator Directory Import command.

The import file can originate from another Exchange Server using the **Directory Export** command (which I'll discuss in a moment) or from a foreign email system. The format must be comma-delimited.

You can create new Windows NT accounts based on the user field or delete existing Windows NT accounts.

Deleted Accounts Are Unrecoverable   Be careful when selecting the Delete Windows NT Account option. There is no Undo function for object deletion.

The logging level can be None, Low, or High. The high-level logging is the most detailed and will show a direct mapping from the import file to the container.

If the foreign email system you are attempting to import from doesn't use Microsoft standard delimiters, you can use the **Separator** field to customize the characters.

The Multivalued Properties option is important if you are interested in ensuring the unique email addresses (such as MSMail and SMTP) are not overwritten.

Directory Export. This command is used to create a comma-separated file for importing into another Exchange site or foreign email system. You'll use this command most often when moving users from one site to another or setting up a foreign email gateway.

As Figure 6.18 displays, you have complete control over the export process. You can specify which MS Exchange Server to run the import process on and which Home Server to extract the data from.

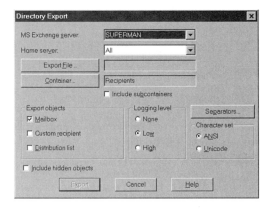

FIGURE 6.18   The Exchange Administrator Directory Export command.

Specify the export file by using the **Export File** option, you can also specify the characters used as separators by selecting the **Separator** option. Note that Exchange's **Directory Import** command calls for a comma-delimited file.

The **Export File**, **Logging Level**, and **Separator** options function the same as in **Directory Import**, which you just covered.

You can filter which objects to include in the export by selecting the appropriate option in the **Export Objects** section. Note that you can include hidden objects if you need to.

The last option is useful for characters>importing between various operating systems. You can use either *ANSI* characters or *Unicode*.

 ANSI   An acronym for the American National Standards Institute. This organization sets standards for the computer industry. ANSI characters are standard, 8-bit text characters used by any computer system. Examples are letters and numbers.

Unicode   Also a standard for text, but instead of ANSI characters that uses 8 bits to define characters, Unicode uses 16 bits. For Western-based languages such as English and French, 8 bits are enough, but for Chinese and Japanese 16 bits are needed.

Extract Windows NT Account List. This command is typically used to propagate a new Exchange server with existing users.

Figure 6.19 displays the options available when you perform this export procedure. You need to specify the domain and domain controller you will be exporting information from. The comma-delimited file created during the export procedure can be specified with the **Output Filename** option. You will need to **Browse** the directory structure before inputting a filename.

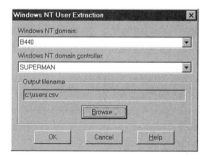

FIGURE **6.19**   The Exchange Administrator Extract Windows NT Account List command.

When the export is complete, the command will respond with any errors that were encountered.

Extract NetWare Account List. The Extract NetWare Account List is a very useful command when migrating from Novell NetWare to Windows NT Server.

The command's options, displayed in Figure 6.20, are fairly simple to configure.

FIGURE **6.20**   The Exchange Administrator Extract NetWare Account List command.

The name of the NetWare server you want to extract accounts from needs to be specified. In addition, you will need to specify an administrator-level username and password.

The comma-delimited file created during the export procedure can be specified with the Output Filename option. You might need to **Browse** the directory structure before inputting a filename.

NDS Not Supported   The Extract NetWare Account List command doesn't support Novell Directory Services (NDS). NDS is a naming directory service used by NetWare Servers to track network objects. The command does support Bindery objects, which are typically found on NetWare 3.x servers.

Find Recipients. Even though Exchange Administrator does a good job of allowing you to filter and sort information, you might still have difficulty finding certain objects. This will be true as your organization grows and adds more and more users and distribution lists.

The Find Recipients command is a powerful tool for helping you find the recipients you need quickly. As shown in Figure 6.21, you have detailed control over which fields to use in your search.

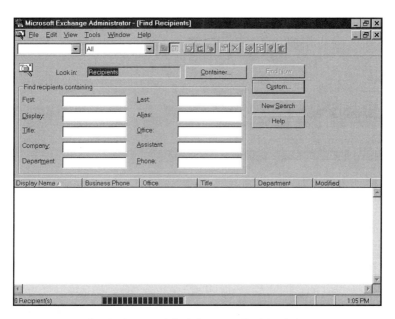

FIGURE 6.21   The Exchange Administrator Find Recipients command.

You can start the Find Recipients process by specifying the container in which to search by using the **Container** option. After you specify the container, you can enter a specific data into the search fields. When you have entered your search criteria, you can click **Find Now**, and all the recipients matching the criteria are displayed in the results pane. You can then modify the recipients directly from the results pane.

Narrow Your Find Recipients Searches The Find Recipients command doesn't support wildcards, but it does allow you to specify the first characters of an entry to search. For example, if you want to list all recipients with the last name beginning with R you would enter **R** in the Last field. You would receive the example recipients Richards, Roberts, and Rudman. If you only want to list users beginning with RI, you would enter **RI** in the Last field. Your results might be Richards, but not Rudman.

Among the more configurable aspects of Exchange are the Custom Attributes fields. MS allows you to propagate 10 custom fields with your own information. You might want to enter social security numbers, positions on the company softball team, and so on. The Find Recipients command allows you to search these fields as well.

When you want to clear the results from a prior search and complete a different search, click the New Search option.

Move Mailbox. This command is the biggest disappointment of the Exchange Administrator program. To use the command, select a recipient object, click **Tools, Move Mailbox.** You can then select a new server for the object. The problem is that you can only move recipient objects between servers on the same site. If you want to move someone from one site to another, you have to use alternative methods, such as notifying the user to save all messages into an offline mailbox (PST file). Then you can use the Directory Export and Import commands to transfer the users directory information.

Add to Address Book View. This command is useful when you publish multiple Address Books. For instance, if your company is linked through a gateway to a vendor, you can publish only the addresses you would like to the vendor's Address Book.

Clean Mailbox. After your Exchange server has been running for a long period of time, you will want to do some maintenance. Part of the maintenance should be cleaning users' mailboxes. The Clean Mailbox command allows you to accomplish this.

As seen in Figure 6.22, the **Clean Mailbox** command does more than prune messages based on date.

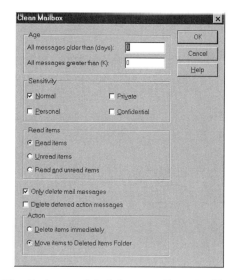

FIGURE **6.22**   The Exchange Administrator Clean Mailbox command.

You can delete messages based on date, size, and even on sensitivity. This is a great feature for leaving important messages, but deleting standard broadcast messages that might not be so vital.

You gain further control by selecting messages to delete based on the read status. You can select read, unread, or both types of messages to delete.

The two most important options to consider are **Only Delete Mail Messages** and **Delete Deferred Action Messages**. The delete mail messages option limits your cleaning efforts to mail messages and not contacts or appointments. The Delete Deferred Action Messages choice limits your cleaning efforts to messages that are not affected by Inbox rules.

When you decided to clean users' mailboxes, you can either delete the messages from the system or move the messages to the user's Deleted Items folder. After they are moved to the Deleted Items folder, the user needs to issue an **Empty Deleted Items Folder** command to actually delete the messages.

Notify Users of Deletion Policy   Ensure your email policy states that messages will be deleted at certain intervals during the year. Nothing is worse than performing maintenance and realizing no one knew messages were going to be deleted. If users would like to keep older messages, they can create a personal folder and store the messages *offline*.

 Offline Message Storing   This allows a user to specify a local or network drive on which they can store their mail. Typically, mail is stored on the Microsoft Exchange 5.5 Server. By using offline storage, remote users can keep their information with them and work when they are not attached to the Microsoft Exchange 5.5 Server.

Start Monitor. This command is simple; when you select a server or link monitor and click **Start Monitor**, the monitoring process begins.

Track Message. One of the more advanced troubleshooting commands, Track Messages allows you to trace the route a message follows through your MS installation.

When you select the **Track Message** command, you're prompted for the server you would like to administer. After you select the server, the Select Message to Track dialog box appears, as shown in Figure 6.23.

Forms Administrator. This command allows you to manage *form libraries*. These are collections of forms for use on the Exchange Server. You can add new libraries, modify existing libraries, and assign permissions.

Newsgroup Hierarchies. This command allows you to convert existing public folders to a newsgroup hierarchy, which is useful for allowing non-Outlook clients access to the folders.

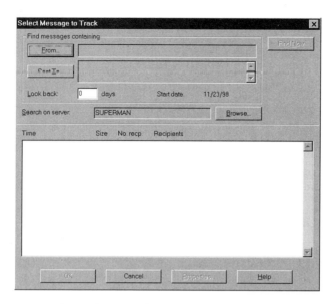

FIGURE 6.23   The Exchange Administrator Track Message command.

Save Connections on Exit. When you exit Exchange Administrator while connected to multiple Exchange servers, Exchange Administrator will save your connection settings, which is great if you administer multiple servers. This command is either enabled or disabled; a check mark indicates the command is toggled on.

Save Connections Now. This command allows you to save your current server connections without having to exit. You would use this command when you finalize your connection list.

Customize Toolbar. This command allows you to add icons and commands to your Exchange Administrator toolbar. This is a powerful tool that allows you to keep frequently used commands a mouse click away.

Figure 6.24 shows the easy-to-use interface for modifying your command bar. You simply use drag and drop to add and remove options.

Options. This command is actually a dialog box with three distinct configuration tabs: **Auto Naming, Permissions,** and **File Format.**

Figure 6.25 shows the Auto Naming option. Auto Naming allows you to control how the display names and aliases are formatted when a new Exchange Mailbox is created.

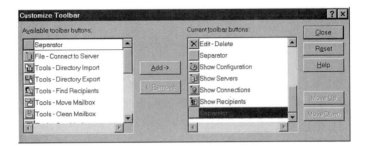

FIGURE 6.24   The Exchange Administrator Customize Toolbar command.

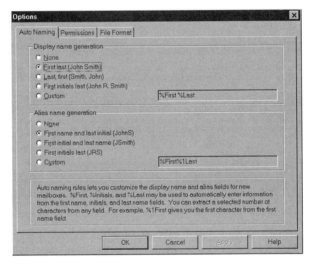

FIGURE 6.25   The Exchange Administrator—Setting the Auto Name configuration.

The Permissions tab of the Options command, shown in Figure 6.26, allows you to set Domain Defaults and Permission Display options for Exchange objects—by default, the permission tabs do not appear for all Exchange objects; permissions are inherited froman objects parent container.

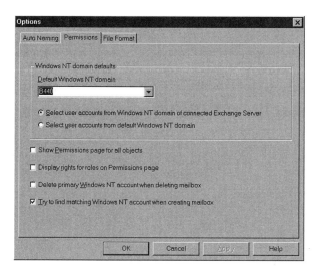

FIGURE 6.26   The Exchange Administrator—Permissions configuration.

If you do many imports or exports, you will appreciate the File Format tab of the Options command, as shown in Figure 6.27 because you can modify the delimiters used to format data on imports and exports. Of course, when you actually do an import or export, you can override these defaults if necessary.

THE WINDOW MENU

The Window menu features standard Windows-compliant menu commands. You can Tile, Cascade, Refresh, and open a New Window, which will effectively create a copy of the window already open for ease of configuration.

THE HELP MENU

The Help menu also features your typical standard Windows commands.

One command you might be asked to choose from the Help menu is About. This command will display a dialog box detailing the version of Exchange Administrator, complete with build number.

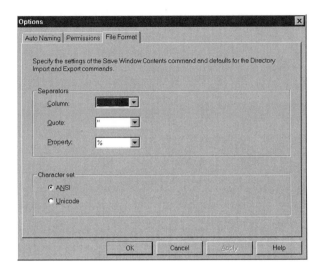

FIGURE 6.27   The Exchange Administrator—File Format configuration.

You can also click the **System Information** button to display information about your Windows NT Server configuration. You might need this information for support purposes.

In this lesson, you learned about the arsenal of commands you have at your disposal when running Exchange Administrator. In the next lesson, you'll learn how to install Outlook 98 and test your Exchange configuration.

LESSON 7

INSTALLING AND TESTING EXCHANGE FUNCTIONS

In this lesson, you'll install and configure the Outlook client. You'll also test the Microsoft Exchange 5.5 installation to ensure you can send and receive messages.

OUTLOOK 98, THE NEXT GENERATION CLIENT

Prior to Microsoft Exchange Server 5.5, there were multiple Exchange clients that shipped with Microsoft Exchange. The older clients are briefly discussed in Lesson 3, "Microsoft Exchange 5.5 Client(s)". These clients are still available from Microsoft and are a good choice if you have users who still use DOS or Windows 3.x.

In today's Microsoft Exchange 5.5 Server world though, the preferred client Microsoft recommends is Outlook 98. As you learned in Lesson 3, Outlook 98 is more than an email client—it is a Personal Information Manager (PIM).

What makes Outlook 98 different from the older Exchange clients is functionality. In the older Exchange clients, you had the ability to send and receive messages. You could also schedule meetings and appointments with a separate application, Schedule+. With Outlook 98, you can still send and receive mail messages, but the meeting and appointment functions are integrated. What makes Outlook 98 the next generation client is the additional functionality it brings to the table. You have an integrated, complete solution for organizing information and accessing the advanced features of Microsoft Exchange 5.5.

Outlook 98 sports the following features not found in the older Exchange clients:

- Integrated meeting and appointment scheduling through the Calendar function

- Superior contacts management through the Contacts function

- Task management for tracking your to-do lists or project deliverables using the Tasks function

- Contact tracking and management using the Journal function

- Free-form note collection with electronic sticky notes through the Notes function.

OTHER VERSIONS OF OUTLOOK

There are two other versions of the Outlook client that offer more limited functionality. Outlook Express and Outlook Web Access use a similar interface as Outlook 98, but do not offer the same wide range of features.

Outlook Express ships with Microsoft Internet Explorer and handles Internet email only. The only method of connecting to an Exchange server is through the use of an Internet standard protocol, such as POP3.

Outlook Web Access allows a user with any browser to access a Microsoft Exchange 5.5 Server and only access their email account and public folders. To use Outlook Web Access, the Microsoft Exchange 5.5 Server needs to be available to an Internet Information Server (IIS) for Web page serving.

MODES, SERVICES, AND PROFILES

Configuring Outlook 98 is sometimes confusing, as it supports three distinct connectivity modes: Stand Alone, Internet, and Corporate (or Workgroup).

Stand Alone mode allows Outlook 98 to work as a very powerful PIM, but doesn't allow for the connectivity or Workgroup features.

Internet mode brings the full power of Outlook 98 with the PIM features to your computer, but lacks the capability to connect to a Microsoft Exchange 5.5 Server. You can connect to other email servers, Exchange included, using Internet based protocols. This allows you to send and receive email.

Corporate or Workgroup mode offers full PIM functionality and allows you to connect to a Microsoft Exchange Server 5.5. Using this mode, you can send and receive email and also access the advanced workgroup features of Microsoft Exchange 5.5.

Outlook 98 uses configuration files called *services* to determine how and where to process email. Services are designed modularly, so you can plug one or more in if your installation calls for it. For instance, you can run the Microsoft Exchange service allowing you to connect to the Microsoft Exchange 5.5 Server for mail in addition to running the Personal Folders service allowing you to store mail messages offline.

Each of the services you choose, as well as other Outlook 98 configuration information, is stored in a *profile*. A profile is a collection of services and configuration settings for an Outlook 98 session. You can use multiple profiles for testing, using Outlook 98 remotely, or for changing account names.

WHAT YOU NEED TO RUN OUTLOOK 98

You need to take the official Outlook 98 system requirements shown in Table 7.1 skeptically. Remember, Microsoft is only saying these requirements are to load the program and run it. It could be painfully slow, but it functions. The following table walks through Microsoft's minimum requirements and the real-world functional specifications. Your pain threshold might be higher, so you could accept something less than the requirements I recommend.

TABLE 7.1   MINIMUM OUTLOOK 98 SYSTEM REQUIREMENTS

	MICROSOFT SUGGESTED	REAL WORLD
Processor	486/66MHz	Pentium 100MHz
Memory	Windows 95; 8MB	Windows 95; 16MB
	Windows NT; 16MB	Windows NT; 32MB
Operating systems	Windows 9X or Windows NT 4 with Service Pack 3	Windows 9X or Windows NT 4 with Service Pack 3

Outlook 98 also needs Internet Explorer 4.0 or above to be installed. Internet Explorer doesn't have to be your default browser, but the components must be installed. If Internet Explorer 3.0 or below is currently installed, it will be upgraded when you install Outlook 98.

The Internet Explorer components provide the HTML and other rendering services to Outlook 98. Unlike the older Exchange clients, Outlook 98 provides full HTML mail compatibility.

There are three installation options for Outlook 98. Each brings a level of functionality to your Outlook 98 installation, but also consumes more hard drive space.

 Patch Your Office 97 Before Outlook 98   Office 97 Users: Microsoft strongly recommends that you install the downloaded Office 97 SR-1 patch prior to installing Outlook 98. Upgrading to Office 97 SR-1 after installing Outlook 98 requires a full reinstallation of Office 97 and the SR-1 module.

INSTALLATION OPTIONS AND SIZES

According to Microsoft there are three installation options for Outlook 98:

- **Minimum**—Installs core Outlook 98 files (including Internet Explorer 4.01, Microsoft VM for Java, and multimedia enhancements). Recommended for users who have hard disk space constraints.

- **Standard**—Installs everything included with Minimum, plus the Outlook Help files. This is my recommended installation option.

- **Full**—Installs everything included with Standard, plus Database Converters, Development Tools, Microsoft NetMeeting™, and Outlook enhancements (such as Office sounds, animated cursors, and the Lotus Organizer converter). Recommended for developers.

Each of the choices will have an impact on how much hard drive space is needed. The amount of space needed is called a *footprint*. Keep in mind the footprint is the number of megabytes needed to install the software, not necessarily to run it.

According to Microsoft, your computer has one of three configurations:

• Internet Explorer 4.01 and Outlook 97 are already on your computer

• Internet Explorer 4.01 (but not Outlook 97) is already on your computer

• Neither Internet Explorer 4.01 nor Outlook 97 are on your computer

Microsoft provides two hard drive sizes for each installation and configuration option.

• **Installed disk size**—This is the size of the application on your computer, after you are done installing. Also known as the footprint. This number excludes setup and backup files.

• **Free Space needed for installation**—This is the amount of space necessary on your hard drive, in order to run the Setup program. It is larger than the final installed disk size, because the final footprint utilizes compression technology.

Based on which installation option you selected and the current state of your computer, download size and hard drive space requirements are shown in Table 7.2.

TABLE 7.2   INSTALLATION DISK SPACE REQUIREMENTS

WHAT'S ON YOUR COMPUTER	INSTALLED DISK SIZE (FOOTPRINT)	FREE SPACE NEEDED FOR INSTALLATION
Minimum		
Internet Explorer 4.01 and Outlook 97	22MB	34MB
Internet Explorer 4.01 (but not Outlook 97)	39MB	55MB

continues

TABLE 7.2   CONTINUED

WHAT'S ON YOUR COMPUTER	INSTALLED DISK SIZE (FOOTPRINT)	FREE SPACE NEEDED FOR INSTALLATION
Minimum		
No Internet Explorer 4.01 or Outlook 97	65MB	102MB
Standard		
Internet Explorer 4.01 and Outlook 97	22MB	37MB
Internet Explorer 4.01 (but not Outlook 97)	41MB	57MB
No Internet Explorer 4.01 or Outlook 97	68MB	104MB
Full		
Internet Explorer 4.01 and Outlook 97	32MB	52MB
Internet Explorer 4.01 (but not Outlook 97)	53MB	75MB
No Internet Explorer 4.01 or Outlook 97	81MB	121MB

INSTALLING OUTLOOK 98

You have two choices when installing Outlook 98. You can install the product from the Web or from CD-ROM. The Web installation is very time-consuming unless you have a high-speed connection to the Internet. It is also very confusing for someone who is not accustomed to Outlook. I'll cover the CD-ROM installation for simplicity purposes. The installation for this lesson assumes that you have Internet Explorer 4.0 or above installed and that you have never installed Outlook 97.

Insert the Outlook 98 CD-ROM into your CD-ROM drive and select the
Start menu. Click **Run** and then type `D:\OUTLK98\SETUP.EXE` where D: is
the drive letter of your CD-ROM. The introductory Outlook 98 installation screen will appear, as shown in Figure 7.1.

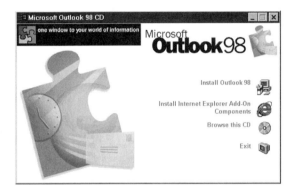

FIGURE **7.1**   The Introductory Outlook 98 screen is your roadmap
for installation.

You should select **Install Outlook 98**, which opens the Outlook 98
Installation Wizard, as shown in Figure 7.2.

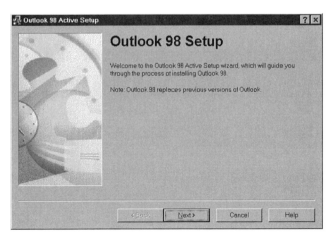

FIGURE **7.2**   The Outlook 98 Wizard guides you through the
installation process.

Clicking **Next** will present the license agreement screen shown in Figure 7.3.

FIGURE **7.3**   The Outlook 98 License Agreement screen.

After agreeing to the license details, you will be asked for your username and organization, as shown in Figure 7.4. This information is not your Microsoft Exchange 5.5 account or Windows NT account; this name is used for reference.

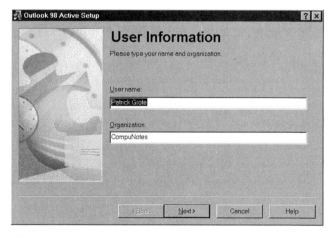

FIGURE **7.4**   Entering your username and organization.

After you enter your username and organization, the Installation Option screen appears, as shown in Figure 7.5. This is the option you choose if you want either the Minimal, Standard, or Full installation, as previously discussed. The default value is Standard, which I will choose for this example installation.

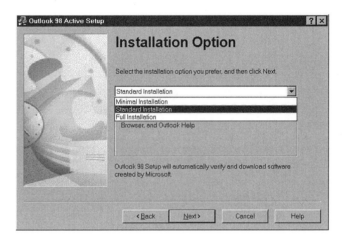

FIGURE 7.5   Selecting your installation option in Outlook 98.

You're prompted to enter a destination for the files. Accept the program defaults and click **Next**. The Outlook 98 installation process then prepares to install Outlook 98, as shown in Figure 7.6.

The Outlook 98 installation process prompts you to decide whether you would like to upgrade currently installed products or reinstall them. Typically you would select **Upgrade Only Newer Items**, as shown in Figure 7.7. You would select **Reinstall All Components** if you were having an issue with the installation process.

After you have selected **Upgrade Only Newer Items**, the Outlook 98 installation process continues to prepare for the installation.

As the installation progresses, you will see a status indicator, as shown in Figure 7.8.

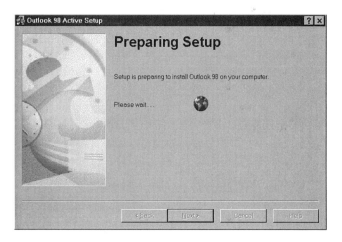

FIGURE **7.6**   The Outlook 98 installation process prepares to install Outlook 98.

FIGURE **7.7**   Deciding whether to upgrade or reinstall components.

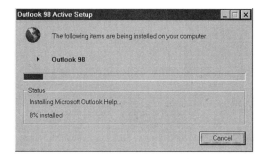

FIGURE **7.8**   Watching the progress of the Outlook installation.

When the installation process is complete you will be prompted to restart your machine, as shown in Figure 7.9. Select **OK** and your computer will restart.

FIGURE 7.9   Restarting the computer after the Outlook installation is complete.

TESTING THE MICROSOFT EXCHANGE 5.5 INSTALLATION

After Outlook 98 is successfully installed, you need to test the Microsoft Exchange 5.5 installation. A client such as Outlook 98 is not very much help if you don't have an active account on the Microsoft Exchange 5.5 Server. Your first step in testing the installation is to create a user account.

 Know Your Rights   To create a user account, you must have adequate rights in the domain where the Microsoft Exchange 5.5 Server resides.

Run the Windows NT Server User Manager for Domains program by selecting **Start, Programs, Administrative Tools (common)**, and **User Manager for Domains**. The following steps will create a test user called *Lex Luther*:

1. Select **New User** from the **User** menu.

2. Add information to each field with the proper values as shown in Figure 7.10. Enter **PASSWORD** as the user password.

> **Don't Be So Sensitive**   Passwords are not case-sensitive, which is unlike those for UNIX.

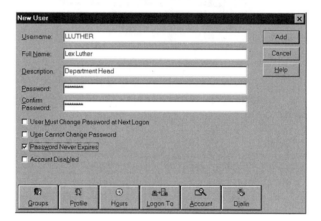

FIGURE 7.10   Creating a test user using the User Manager for domains.

3. Click **Add**. You're then presented with the user's properties screen, as shown in Figure 7.11.

4. Add information to each field with the proper values as shown in Figure 7.12.

5. Click **OK**, and then click **Close**.

Congratulations! You have now created a test user named Lex Luther. You don't need to create the Microsoft Exchange 5.5 mailbox, because the System Attendant has done it for you.

CONFIGURING OUTLOOK 98 FOR USE

You should take a deep breath now, because you will finally launch Outlook 98 and test the Microsoft Exchange 5.5 Server.

Double-click the Outlook 98 icon on your desktop. You will be asked whether you would like to configure a profile for Microsoft Exchange or Microsoft Mail; select Microsoft Exchange.

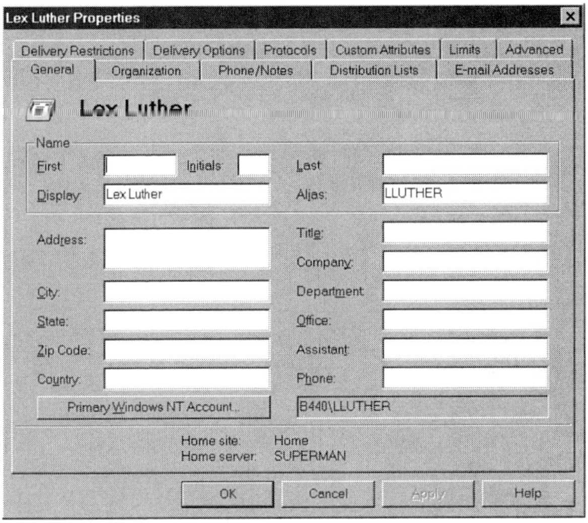

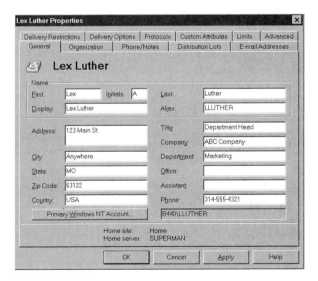

FIGURE **7.11**   The User Properties screen in User Manager for domains.

FIGURE **7.12**   Entering user properties in the User Properties screen.

You will then be prompted for your Microsoft Exchange Server name and Mailbox for your account, as shown in Figure 7.13. Make sure you use your test account name.

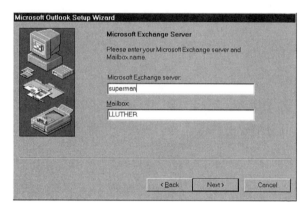

FIGURE 7.13   Creating an Outlook 98 profile.

You will then be asked if you travel with your computer. For testing purposes, select **No**, and then **Next**. Outlook 98 will then go to the Inbox screen.

To send a test message select **File**, **New**, **New Mail Message**, and you will be presented with the New Mail Message dialog box.

To complete testing, follow these instructions:

1. Address your message in the To field to **lluther**.

2. Enter a subject of **TEST MESSAGE**.

3. Enter **TEST** in the body of the message. Your message should appear similar to the one in Figure 7.14.

4. Select the **Send Message** icon.

You should then click the **Send and Receive** button on top of the Outlook 98 button bar. If your installation was successful, you will receive your test message. Congratulations! Your installation of Outlook 98 was successful.

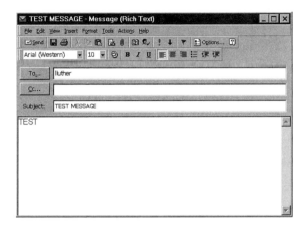

FIGURE 7.14 Sending a test message in Outlook 98.

In this lesson, you've seen how to install Outlook 98 and configure it to work with your Exchange 5.5 Server. In the following lesson, you'll learn how to send mail using a variety of Exchange clients.

LESSON 8

TRANSFERRING MAIL WITH OTHER MICROSOFT EXCHANGE 5.5 SERVERS

In this lesson, you'll learn how to transfer mail with Microsoft Exchange 5.5 servers on one site or multiple sites.

Communication between Microsoft Exchange 5.5 servers can be classified as *intrasite* or *intersite*.

Intrasite communications occur when the Microsoft Exchange 5.5 servers communicating are in the same site.

Intersite communications occur when the Microsoft Exchange 5.5 servers communicating are in different sites.

INTRASITE COMMUNICATIONS

When two Microsoft Exchange 5.5 servers in the same site need to transfer information, the Mail Transfer Agent (MTA) or Directory Service (DS) is used.

Using a Remote Procedure Call (RPC) to communicate, the information is directly transferred in its native form from one server to another.

Servers within a site are considered to be local to each other and connected via an available and high-speed network link.

INTERSITE COMMUNICATIONS

When connecting Microsoft Exchange 5.5 servers from different sites, you need a reliable, effective method of communication. Microsoft meets these requirements with *connectors*. Connectors are akin to routers on a network. The connector links one Microsoft Exchange 5.5 Server to another one through various methods.

During site-to-site connections, information is passed using the MTA. The Directory Services are not involved. DS information is placed in an email message, delivered through the connector by the MTA, and processed on the destination server.

There are four messaging connectors supported by Microsoft Exchange 5.5 Server:

1. **Site Connector**—Uses the internal Microsoft Exchange 5.5 MTA to transfer information directly to other Microsoft Exchange servers. Figure 8.1 demonstrates the flow of email through a site connector.

2. **X.400 Connector**—Uses the X.400 standard to transfer information. Information is converted to an X.400 compliant mail message before transfer. Figure 8.2 demonstrates the flow of email through a X.400 connector.

3. **Internet Mail Service**—Using SMTP, Microsoft Exchange 5.5 can transfer information over the Internet. Figure 8.3 shows the process of using SMTP to deliver email.

Site Connector

Site A

Microsoft Exchange 5.5
Server Accounting

Microsoft Exchange 5.5
Server MIS

Microsoft Exchange 5.5
Server Marketing

Microsoft Exchange 5.5
Server Distribution

Site B

Microsoft Exchange 5.5
Server Art

Microsoft Exchange 5.5
Server IT

Microsoft Exchange 5.5
Server Production

Microsoft Exchange 5.5
Server Packaging

Figure 8.1   The site connector delivers messages directly to the recipient server.

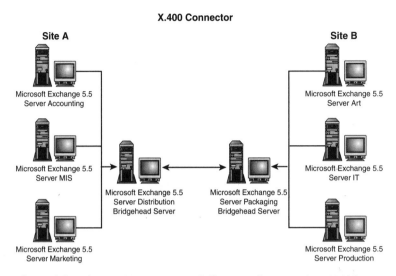

Figure 8.2   The X.400 connector delivers mail to another X.400 connector

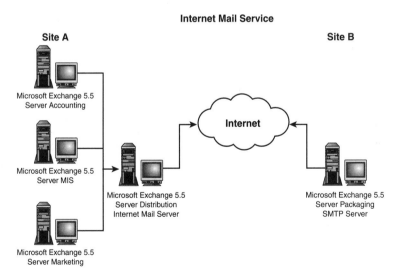

Figure 8.3   Microsoft Exchange 5.5 messages can be routed using SMTP.

4. **Dynamic RAS Connector**—Uses RAS to transfer information
   between sites without a permanent connection. Figure 8.4 shows
   the dynamic RAS connector linking to another dynamic RAS
   connector.

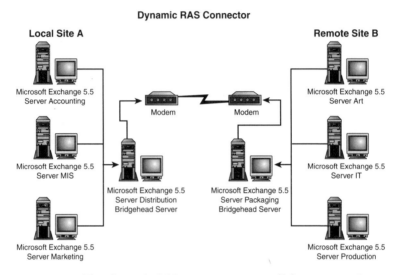

Figure 8.4   The dynamic RAS connector uses a dial-up connection
to transfer email

SITE CONNECTOR

Using RPC for site-to-site communications, the site connector is the most
efficient method of connecting two Microsoft Exchange 5.5 sites. RPC
doesn't require any protocols to transmit and receive information.
Messages being delivered through the site connector aren't translated
from one format to another, so time is saved. The message's native
Exchange format is used.

Site connectors require a dedicated, higher bandwidth connection of at
least 128K or above. The site connector is a bandwidth hog and will
attempt to consume all available bandwidth. You cannot limit messages by
size.

Traffic Jam   Microsoft Exchange 5.5 uses as much bandwidth as it can when communicating with other sites. If your remote site is connected via modem, you shouldn't choose a modem with a throughput rate of less that 33.6kbps.

 No Routing for Me, Please   Each Microsoft Exchange 5.5 Server with a site connector can route mail. In particularly busy sites, you might want to designate only one Microsoft Exchange 5.5 Server to route via the site connector. You can do this by creating a *Bridgehead server*. A Bridgehead server is a server where all the outgoing and incoming messages are funneled for delivery. Figure 8.2 demonstrates the Bridgehead concept.

X.400 CONNECTOR

The X.400 connector cannot deliver mail to individual servers, but must use a Bridgehead server. You can use X.400 connectors to limit the size of the messages and the time in which they can be sent.

The X.400 connector is well suited for low-bandwidth, dedicated connections such as a 56K frame relay line or a 64K ISDN connection. You can limit the amount of bandwidth used, so Microsoft Exchange 5.5 won't consume all available bandwidth.

The X.400 connector can be used to not only connect to other Exchange servers in other sites, but also other X.400-based email systems.

The X.400 connector is slower than the site connector for three reasons:

1. **Protocol Usage**—X.400 doesn't use RPC to transfer mail. X.400 relies on TCP/IP or variants thereof.

2. **Bridgehead**—X.400 can't deliver mail directly to a recipient Microsoft Exchange 5.5 Server. You need to use a Bridgehead server, which can delay delivery based on the usage of the server.

3. **Translation**—X.400 needs the Microsoft Exchange 5.5 message in its own format. This requires a translation process that can consume resources and delay delivery.

INTERNET MAIL SERVICE

The Internet Mail Service is based on the Simple Mail Transfer Protocol (SMTP). SMTP is the core protocol used for mail delivery on the Internet. By using the Internet Mail Service, Microsoft Exchange Server 5.5 can deliver messages between sites using SMTP.

The Internet Mail Service is a good choice if an existing SMTP backbone and DNS servers are installed. The Internet Mail Service is highly configurable.

We'll handle the Internet Mail Server in Lesson 9,"The Internet Mail Service."

DYNAMIC RAS CONNECTOR

The dynamic RAS connector is used to connect two sites over a dial-up connection. The connection can be analog or ISDN.

In the process of designing a Microsoft Exchange 5.5 infrastructure, you should keep in mind that dynamic RAS connectors require some forethought:

- Because dynamic RAS connectors require more configuration than other connectors, it might take more time to test and install.

- Dynamic RAS connectors send messages in X.400 format that might lead to an additional delay.

- Because the dynamic RAS connector has the additional responsibility of manager calls in and out of the server, additional resources will be necessary. The additional processing necessary is dependent on the load the dynamic RAS connector will carry.

CHOOSING THE PROPER CONNECTOR

Choosing a Microsoft Exchange 5.5 connector for intersite communications is as much an art as it is a science. Depending on your situation, any of the connectors will work. The question is, will they work efficiently?

Table 8.1 illustrates the differences in connector requirements and performance; use it as a reference when deciding which connector to utilize.

TABLE 8.1   CONNECTOR OPTIONS

CONFIGURATION OPTION	SITE CONNECTOR	X.400	INTERNET MAIL SERVICE	DYNAMIC RAS CONNECTOR
Protocols Used	RPC	TCP/IP and Variants	TCP/IP	TCP/IP, NetBEUI, Nwlink
Bandwidth Recommendation	Dedicated 128K and greater	Dedicated 64K and greater	Dedicated 33.6KK and greater	Dial-up only
Message Format	Native Exchange	X.400	SMTP	X.400
Bridgehead Requirement	Optional	Required	Optional	Required
Message Size Restriction	No	Yes	Yes	Yes
User Access Restriction	No	Yes	Yes	Yes

In this lesson, you learned how to use Microsoft Exchange to transfer mail among other Exchange servers and other types of email systems. In the next lesson, you'll learn how to install the Internet Mail Service.

LESSON 9

THE INTERNET MAIL SERVICE

In this lesson, you'll cover the Internet Mail Service, which allows you to communicate with the Internet. The functions, protocols, and configuration options associated with it are also covered.

Would you like the ability to send messages to anyone, anywhere in the world instantly and reliably? If you have an Internet connection at your company, Microsoft Exchange 5.5, coupled with the Internet Mail Service can give you this ability.

The Internet is a vast collection of connected networks just like yours. Each of these networks might have an email server like your Microsoft Exchange 5.5 server. Sending messages between these sites is an easy way to communicate and transfer files. Microsoft Exchange 5.5 includes the Internet Mail Service, which gives your server the capability to become part of the Internet community instead of an isolated island.

TALKING WITH THE WORLD

In order to communicate with the other email servers on the Internet, you'll need to speak their language. Just as a language is defined by communicating with certain groups of people, a protocol is the computers' version of a language—it lets computers communicate with each other. Microsoft Exchange 5.5 supports the most common email-related Internet *protocols*. The protocols can be categorized as *client* and *server* side protocols. Client protocols are used to connect a client to the Microsoft Exchange 5.5 Server for the purpose of sending and receiving information. Server protocols are used to facilitate sending and receiving information from resources on the Internet.

Protocol   When two computers need to communicate with each other, an agreed upon format for transferring the data is necessary. This is the protocol. The protocol is a common method for transmitting information from one computer to another.

Microsoft Exchange 5.5 supports the following client protocols:

- **POP3**—The Post Office Protocol 3 (POP3) is used by the client to retrieve email from a server. POP3 supports only very basic features.

- **IMAP4**—Some clients use Internet Message Access Protocol 4 to retrieve email from a server. IMAP4 supports advanced features such as keyword searching and selective message retrieval.

- **LDAP**—Lightweight Directory Access protocol is used by the client to obtain directory information, such as email addresses, from email servers.

- **HTTP**—Hypertext Transfer Protocol is used by the client to access Web server front ends that connect to servers. Outlook Web Access requires HTTP.

Microsoft Exchange 5.5 supports the following server protocols:

- **NNTP**—Network News Transport Protocol is the server-based protocol used to post, distribute, and retrieve Usenet (newsgroup) messages. Clients can also use NNTP for the same purpose.

- **TCP/IP**—Transmission Control Protocol/Internet Protocol is the server-based protocol for connecting one host to another. After a connection between hosts is made using TCP/IP, another protocol called SMTP can be used to transfer email. Think of TCP/IP as the delivery truck that gets the information to its destination.

- **DNS**—Domain name system is a server-based protocol that contains and manages TCP/IP addresses. When you would like to send a message to, say, `pgrote@compunotes.com`, Microsoft

Exchange 5.5 has no idea where compunotes.com is located on the Internet. DNS resolves the proper name of compunotes.com to the TCP/IP address of 209.100.53.43. Using the TCP/IP address, Microsoft Exchange 5.5 can deliver the message successfully.

 Send to the Right Address Resolving an address is like looking up someone's postal address. If you know someone's name it's like knowing the domain address pgrote@compunotes.com. To find the postal address for someone, you could look up his or her last name in the phone book. It's a similar process for finding a domain name's TCP/IP address. Instead of using a phonebook, you would use the DNS.

- **SMTP**—Simple Mail Transfer Protocol is a server-based protocol used to deliver mail from one email server to another over the Internet. SMTP is like a mailperson who delivers mail to your mailbox. SMTP acts as a mailperson delivering mail to an email server's mailbox.

HOW THE INTERNET MAIL SERVICE WORKS

The Internet Mail Service is a true Windows NT Server service. This means it runs in the background on your Windows NT Server awaiting commands from the Microsoft Exchange 5.5 Server. Being a service is a benefit, because its usage requires no intervention from the system administrator.

IMS Is not Installed by Default   IMS is not installed during the default Microsoft Exchange 5.5 installation routine. You must install it after your Microsoft Exchange 5.5 installation is complete. You'll cover the installation in more detail later in this lesson.

Microsoft commonly refers to the Internet Mail Service as IMS. The IMS uses three server-based components to receive and route mail to the appropriate destination. The three components are TCP/IP, DNS, and SMTP.

When sending a message to another SMTP email server, IMS begins by querying the DNS to resolve the domain name. The DNS contains the Mail Exchange (MX) record for the domain name. The MX record points to the mail server for the domain in question. After DNS returns the TCP/IP address found in the MX record for the SMTP server, IMS uses TCP/IP to open a communication line with the SMTP email server. With the communication line open, IMS uses SMTP to begin a transfer session with the remote SMTP server. Barring any problems, the email is transferred and the communication line is closed. Figure 9.1 illustrates this process.

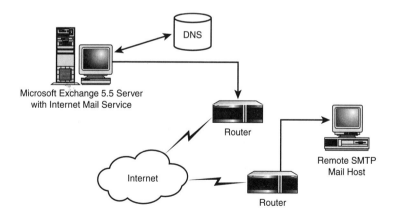

FIGURE 9.1   The IMS process of routing messages to the Internet.

INSTALLING THE INTERNET MAIL SERVICE

Installation of the Internet Mail Service is dependent on TCP/IP being installed on your Windows NT Server. To verify that your Windows NT Server is configured for TCP/IP usage, perform the following steps:

1. Select the **Start** menu.

2. Choose **Settings**.

3. Launch the **Control Panel**.

4. When the Control Panel applets appear, select **Network**.

5. After the Network applet loads, select the **Protocols** tab.

6. You should notice that TCP/IP is loaded, as shown in Figure 9.2.

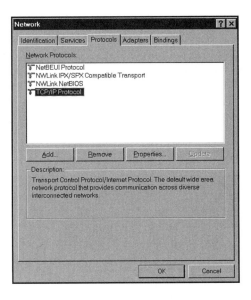

FIGURE 9.2   You can easily verify TCP/IP is loaded.

If TCP/IP is not loaded, you will need to install it. The following directions will successfully install TCP/IP:

1. Select the **Start** menu.

2. Choose **Settings**.

3. Launch the **Control Panel**.

4. When the Control Panel window appears, select **Network**.

5. After the Network applet loads, select the **Protocols** tab.

6. Click the **Add** button and select **TCP/IP Protocol**.

7. You need to enter your TCP/IP address, subnet mask, and default gateway. This information should be obtained from your infrastructure group or your ISP.

8. Select the **DNS** tab and enter your hostname and domain name. Typically, your hostname is the name of the server. For example, the server named MIS in the CompuNotes.com domain would have a hostname MIS.

9. Enter your DNS TCP/IP address.

10. Select **OK**, and then **Close**.

Adding Protocol Might Overwrite Certain Files
When adding a new protocol to your Windows NT 4.0 Server, you might need to use files from the original Windows NT 4.0 Server CD-ROM. If you do this, you'll need to reapply the latest Service Pack. Failure to do so might result in an unstable platform.

There are several configuration items you must know before you install the IMS. The Table 9.1 details what information you need and where you can find it:

TABLE 9.1   CONFIGURATION INFORMATION YOU'LL NEED

WHAT YOU NEED	WHAT IT IS	WHERE TO GET IT
Your company's domain name	Your domain name is similar to CompuNotes.com.	Your ISP will give this to you.

continues

TABLE 9.1   CONTINUED

WHAT YOU NEED	WHAT IT IS	WHERE TO GET IT
DNS server address	The TCP/IP address of the DNS server is in the format of 192.168.0.1.	The DNS TCP/IP address is either provided by your ISP or is the TCP/IP address of your server or router that provides this function on your network. If you are not sure what server provides this, you can type **NSLOOKUP** from the Start, Run command. The address listed is your DNS server's TCP/IP address.
Server on which IMS will be installed	This is the Microsoft Exchange 5.5 Server that will run the IMS.	You should decide which Microsoft Exchange 5.5 Server would host this function. If you have a single Microsoft Exchange 5.5 Server then that is your only choice.
Administrative Account	This account will receive administrative messages from the IMS.	This should be your main Microsoft Exchange 5.5 Administrator.

WHAT YOU NEED	WHAT IT IS	WHERE TO GET IT
Service Account	The service information account you created during the initial Microsoft Exchange 5.5 Server installation is needed for processing.	Refer to Lesson 5, "Installing Microsoft Exchange."

From the Exchange Administrator main screen, select the server you would like to install IMS on and go to the Connections object. Select the **File** menu, choose **New Other**, and click **Internet Mail Service.** You'll be presented with the Internet Mail Wizard dialog box, as shown in Figure 9.3.

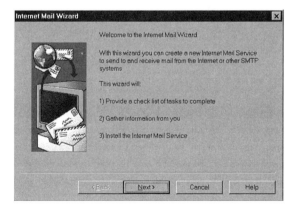

FIGURE **9.3**   Starting the Internet Mail Wizard.

Wizard   An automated installation process that takes your input and configures a selected piece of software based on the information you provide.

Click on **Next** and you'll see that the wizard prompts you to ensure you have configured your Windows NT Server properly. This warning box is displayed in Figure 9.4.

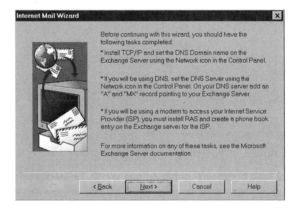

FIGURE **9.4**   The Installation Wizard ensures you have done your homework.

After clicking **Next**, you are the asked which Microsoft Exchange 5.5 Server you would like to install IMS on. You should select the correct server. Additionally, you can specify a dial-up RAS connection to your ISP instead of a dedicated connection. This dialog box is shown in Figure 9.5.

After choosing your Microsoft Exchange 5.5 Server for installation, you are presented with the DNS method configuration screen, as shown in Figure 9.6. If you have your own DNS server, select **Use domain name system (DNS) to send mail**. If you are relying on your ISP to provide this service, enter the TCP/IP address of their DNS server in the **Route all mail through a single host** field.

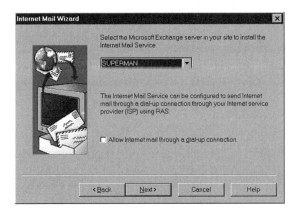

FIGURE **9.5**   Selecting a method for using DNS..

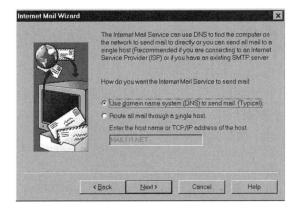

FIGURE **9.6**   Selecting a method for using DNS.

After you select the delivery method, click on **Next**. You will then see the address permission screen shown in Figure 9.7. You can choose to allow email to be sent to any Internet domain name or a selected domain name. You should select **All Internet mail addresses**, unless you are using this connector to move Exchange mail between internal sites.

After making your Internet address permission selection, click **Next**, and you will be shown the site address configuration screen (see Figure 9.8). You will need to enter your domain name, for example
`@Home.CompuNotes.com`.

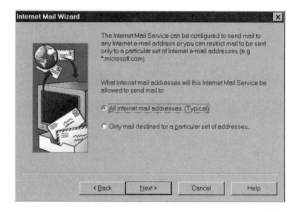

FIGURE 9.7   Setting permissions on Internet addresses.

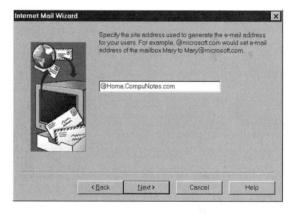

FIGURE 9.8   Setting your domain name for Internet email.

After your domain name is set and you click **Next**, the Internet Mail Wizard prompts you to specify an administrator mailbox. This mailbox should be the mailbox for the Exchange administrator. Accept **Administrator**, as shown in Figure 9.9:

After selecting the administrator account, click on **Next**, and the service account selection screen appears, as shown in Figure 9.10. Enter the password that you chose in Lesson 5, which is for the service account. Enter the information as formatted (remember, passwords are case-sensitive).

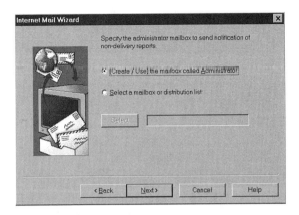

FIGURE 9.9   Setting the administrator account.

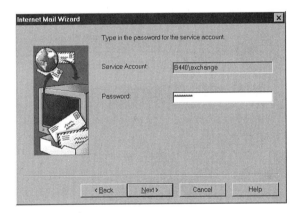

FIGURE 9.10   Setting the service account.

After selecting the service account, click on **Next** and take a deep breath. The Internet Mail Wizard is about to work its magic and create your Internet Mail Service for you. Figure 9.11 shows the informational message that appears before the final step.

While the Internet Mail Wizard works, you will see status messages letting you know what is happening. Occasionally you will be asked to click OK when a service is started. This is normal, so go ahead and click **OK** to continue.

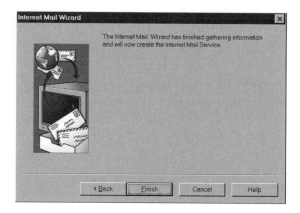

FIGURE 9.11   The wizard works magic.

When the Internet Mail Wizard is completed, the dialog box shown in Figure 9.12 will appear. Your site now has Internet Mail Service! Click on OK after you read the message.

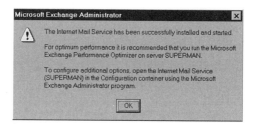

FIGURE 9.12   IMS is now installed.

You have one more important task to complete before you can configure the Internet Mail Service. You should now rerun the Microsoft Exchange Optimizer as you did in Lesson 5. It's important to rerun the Microsoft Exchange Optimizer, so your Microsoft Exchange 5.5 Server functions at its peak potential.

CONFIGURING THE INTERNET MAIL SERVICE

The configuration options for IMS can be intimidating. To keep things simple, you'll be reviewing several screens of information, while only focusing on a few configuration options that a new Exchange Administrator should be aware of.

To begin the configuration process you should use **Exchange Administrator** to open the server on which IMS is installed. Open the **Connections** object and double-click **Internet Mail Service** Figure 9.13 shows the screen that appears.

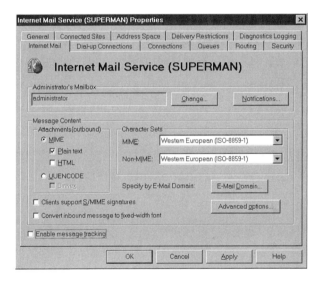

FIGURE 9.13   The Internet Mail Server Internet Mail properties screen.

The main fields to focus on include the following:

- **Administrator's Mailbox**—You can use this option to change the administrator account. This is useful if the main Exchange administrator goes on vacation.

- **Enable Message Tracking**—Message tracking uses the MTA to create a daily log file of the status of each message sent through the IMS. This is a useful tool for troubleshooting.

Select the **Connections** tab, and the configuration screen shown in Figure 9.14 will appear.

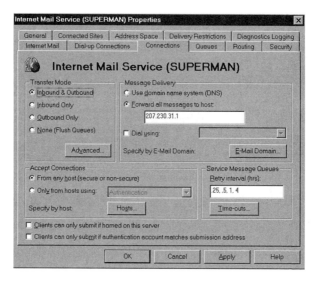

FIGURE 9.14   The Internet Mail Server Connections property screen.

The main fields to focus on in the Connections tab include the following:

- **Transfer Mode**—Transfer mode controls which direction you would like Internet mail to be processed.

- **Message Delivery**—Message delivery controls how your messages get delivered, either via DNS lookups or through a single *smart host*.

- **Service Message Queues**—Service message queues allows you to set the increment of time in which IMS will attempt to transfer email. The **Time-outs** button allows you to set a threshold for retrying undeliverable messages.

- **Accept Connections**—In certain high-security situations, you will want to limit the ability to use IMS unless there is a secure connection.

Now select the **Queues** tab, and that configuration screen, shown in Figure 9.15, will appear.

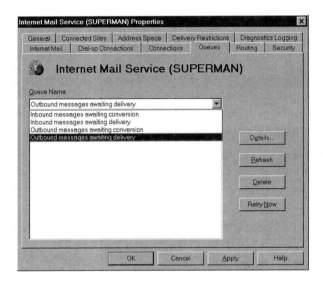

FIGURE **9.15**   The Internet Mail Server Queues configuration screen.

By using this screen, you can actually see what messages are in the IMS queue. You have four sorting options for viewing the messages:

- Inbound Messages Awaiting Conversion

- Inbound Messages Awaiting Delivery

- Outbound Messages Awaiting Conversion

- Outbound Messages Awaiting Delivery

After selecting a sorted view, you can select individual messages, and then either receive details of the message, refresh the message list, delete the message, or retry delivery.

Now, select the General tab to view the configuration screen shown in Figure 9.16.

FIGURE 9.16   The Internet Mail Server General configuration screen.

There is only one field to focus on here:

- **Message Size**—You can limit the size of the IMS message top process; this limitation includes attachments. You should enter the limitation in number of K. Hence, 1 megabyte becomes 1,000K.

Select the Delivery Restrictions tab. You'll see the configuration screen shown in Figure 9.17.

You can prevent users from receiving messages or sending messages through IMS by using this screen. Clicking on the Modify button allows you to specify which users will be limited.

This is a great feature if you have employees who abuse the email service. It also works out well for seasonal or temporary employees.

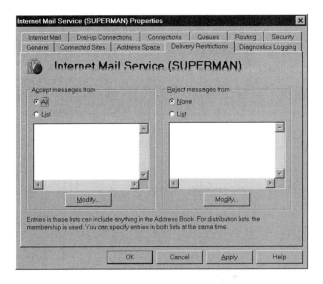

FIGURE 9.17   The Internet Mail Server Delivery Restrictions configuration screen.

That's all the configuration information you will need to address before you can start using the Internet Mail Service.

In this lesson, you learned about the Internet Mail Service: what it is, how it works, how to install it, and how to configure it. In your next lesson, you'll connect Exchange to foreign email systems.

LESSON 10

CONNECTING MICROSOFT EXCHANGE WITH MS MAIL FOR PC NETWORKS

In this lesson, you'll examine the MS Mail email system connector that ships with Microsoft Exchange 5.5. This process is a good example of linking Exchange to other foreign email systems such as MS Mail, GroupWise, cc:Mail, and Lotus Notes.

As you learned in Lesson 8, "Transferring Mail with Other Microsoft Exchange 5.5 Servers," a connector is used to link your Microsoft Exchange 5.5 Server to other Microsoft Exchange servers. You also use connectors to join to foreign email systems.

You just finished detailing the Internet Mail Service that allows you to connect to the Internet in Lesson 9, The Internet Mail Service." Now you'll examine how to connect to foreign email systems that are usually directly connected to your Microsoft Exchange 5.5 Server. The example you'll study is the MS Mail connector.

THE MICROSOFT MAIL CONNECTOR

As you can imagine, connecting Microsoft Exchange 5.5 to older MS Mail servers is easy. Both are Microsoft products and Microsoft has poured years of development effort into the process.

The MS Mail Connector is designed to transfer mail messages to MS Mail from Microsoft Exchange 5.5 that are addressed to MS Mail users. Conversely, the MS Mail Connector transfers mail messages from MS Mail that are addressed to Microsoft Exchange 5.5 users.

The reason that the Microsoft Exchange 5.5 MS Mail Connector works so well is because it uses a shadow MS Mail post office structure.

There are a few steps you must take to prepare your installation for using the MS Mail Connector. They are as follows:

1. Verify the MS Mail Connector is installed on your Microsoft Exchange 5.5 Server. You can do this by using Exchange Administrator and verifying its existence in the Connections object as in Figure 10.1.

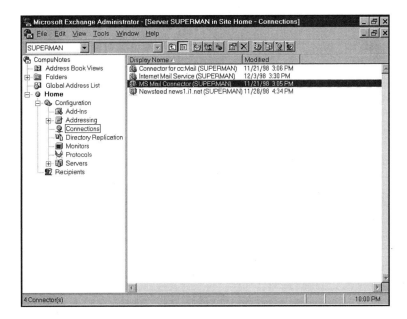

FIGURE 10.1   Verifying the installation of the MS Mail Connector.

2. Document the *UNC* path to existing MS Mail post offices.

UNC   This acronym stands for universal naming convention. It is an easy way to address servers on a network. The syntax is \\server\sharename. If you have an
MS Mail post office on a server called MAIL1 and the
post office is under the share MAILDATA, your UNC
would be \\MAIL1\MAILDATA.

3. Configure each MS Mail post office with an external post office,
   defined as the Microsoft Exchange 5.5 Server.

4. Choose whether you will use the Microsoft Exchange 5.5
   Connector MTA or an existing external MTA.

 Installing the MS Mail Connector   If the MS Mail
Connector is not installed, you will need to rerun the
Microsoft Exchange 5.5 Setup and select Add/Remove.
When prompted select the MS Mail Connector option.

THE MS MAIL CONNECTOR CONFIGURATION SCREENS

There are seven specific screens used to configure the MS Mail
Connector.

INTERCHANGE CONFIGURATION

The Interchange configuration tab, as shown in Figure 10.2, contains the
following configuration options:

- **Administrator's Mailbox**—The MS Mail Connector needs an
  administrator mailbox to serve as a recipient for notifications.
  Ensure you select the person responsible for the MS Mail
  Connector, which is typically the Microsoft Exchange 5.5
  administrator. This is a required field. You will not be able to
  continue configuration without selecting an account.

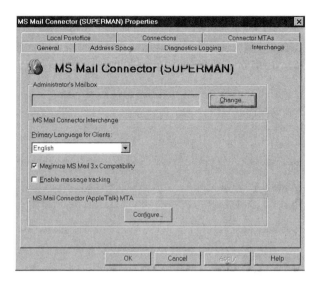

FIGURE 10.2   The MS Mail Connector Interchange tab.

- **Primary Language for Clients**—Select the primary language you want to use. Unless this book has been translated into another language, you should choose English.

- **Maximize MS Mail 3.X Compatibility**—This is an important option for Microsoft Exchange 5.5 and MS Mail interoperability. By selecting this option you ensure that MS Mail users can save and view embedded objects sent from Microsoft Exchange 5.5 clients.

- **Enable Message Tracking**—Message tracking allows you to track each message as it works through the MS Mail Connector. This is a great method for troubleshooting or following a mail routing issue. The log file is stored in \EXCHSRVR\TRACK-ING.LOG.

- **MS Mail Connector (AppleTalk) MTA**—If you have MS Mail for AppleTalk on your network, you will need to configure this option.

AppleTalk Connector Doesn't Refer to Macintosh Clients Keep in mind that the MS Mail Connector (AppleTalk) doesn't refer to MS Mail Macintosh clients. This option refers to the actual MS Mail Server product running on an AppleTalk network. This option affects server-based communications, not clients.

GENERAL CONFIGURATION

The General configuration tab, as shown in Figure 10.3, contains the following configuration options:

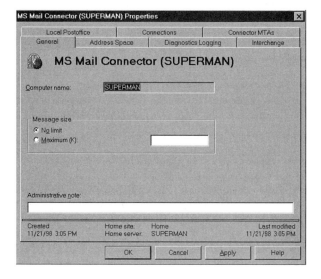

FIGURE 10.3   The MS Mail Connector General tab.

- **Computer Name**—This is a read-only field that identifies which Microsoft Exchange 5.5 Server the MS Mail Connector is installed on.

- **Message Size**—You can choose to allow any size message through the connector, or you can limit the size of the messages. This is helpful for dial-up connections.

- **Administrative Notes**—You have 1,024 characters to say whatever you would like about the MS Mail Connector. Sometimes it is helpful to note recent work completed on the connector.

ADDRESS SPACE

The Address Space configuration tab, as shown in Figure 10.4, allows you to create multiple paths for load balancing and redundancy. By specifying external MS Mail networks, you can ensure messages are routed appropriately.

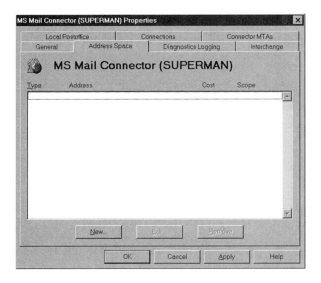

FIGURE **10.4**   The MS Mail Connector Address Space tab.

DIAGNOSTICS LOGGING

The Diagnostics Logging configuration tab, as shown in Figure 10.5, allows you to monitor the performance of the MS Mail Connector.

There are various configuration sections of the Diagnostics Logging tab you will want to consider:

- **MSExchangeMSMI**—This category of diagnostics logs activity between Microsoft Exchange 5.5 and the MS Mail post office structure on the Microsoft Exchange 5.5 Server.

- **MSExchangePCMTA**—This category of diagnostics logs activity between the MS Mail post office structure on the Microsoft Exchange 5.5 Server and other MS Mail post offices through the MS Mail external MTA.

- **MSExchangeATMTA**— This category of diagnostics logs activity between the Microsoft Exchange 5.5 post office structure and the MS Mail for AppleTalk network post offices.

- **Logging Level**—The logging level relates to how much information the MS Mail Connector compiles for tracking. Table 10.1 describes the different levels.

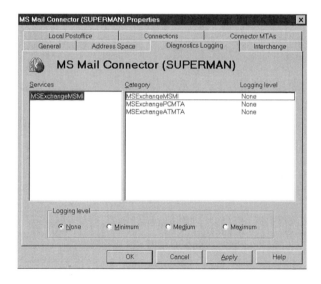

FIGURE **10.5**   The MS Mail Connector Diagnostics Logging tab.

TABLE 10.1   LOGGING LEVELS

LOGGING LEVEL	ACTIVITIES LOGGED
None	Only critical events, error events, and events with a logging level of zero are logged. This is the default level.
Minimum	Events with a logging level of 1 or lower are logged.
Medium	Events with a logging level of 3 or lower are logged.
Maximum	Events with a logging level of 5 or lower are logged.

LOCAL POSTOFFICE

The Local Postoffice configuration tab, as shown in Figure 10.6, contains the following configuration options:

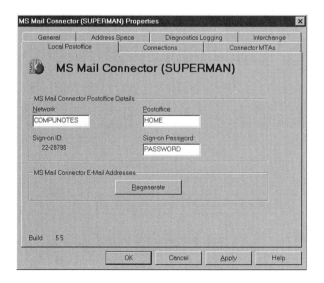

FIGURE 10.6   The MS Mail Connector Local Postoffice tab.

- **MS Mail Connector Postoffice Details**—You can modify the Network, Postoffice, and Sign-on Password if necessary. You cannot modify the Sign-on ID field.

- **MS Mail Connector E-Mail Addresses**—Changing the network or post office names causes regeneration of the MS email address for this site. You will need to run this if you change any MS Mail Connector naming information.

Connections

The Connections configuration tab, as shown in Figure 10.7, allows you to create connections to other MS Mail post offices. You can **Create**, **Modify**, or **Delete** MS Mail post offices. The Queue command is the command you'll use the most. It lists the messages in the Queue to be delivered to that specific post office.

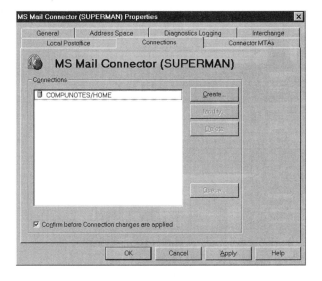

Figure 10.7 The MS Mail Connector Connections tab.

CONNECTOR MTAS

The Connector MTAs configuration tab, as shown in Figure 10.8, allows you to create MTAs to perform the movement of messages from the MS Mail post offices that you defined in the Connections tab.

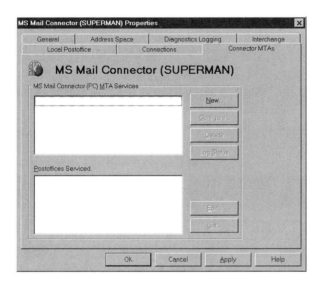

FIGURE 10.8   The MS Mail Connector MTAs tab.

Moving from MS Mail to Microsoft Exchange 5.5 should be your ultimate goal, but if you need to use the MS Mail Connector you can be assured of smooth message delivery during the migration process.

In this lesson, you examined the MS Mail email system connector that ships with Microsoft Exchange 5.5. You can apply this knowledge to link Exchange to other foreign email systems such as MS Mail, GroupWise, cc:Mail, and Lotus Notes.

Lesson 11

Managing Users

In this lesson you'll learn how to manage users through the Exchange Administrator program, and you'll learn about each of the fields associated with users.

If you recall from Lesson 1, "General Concept," Microsoft Exchange 5.5 is based on a scaleable database. Each object in the database can be addressed directly. With this power comes a wide range of configuration options for each user.

You can modify the recipient configuration when you create a new recipient or after the recipient has been created.

To modify the recipient after it is created, you need to select the recipient you would like to modify. Load **Exchange Administrator**, select the **Recipients** container, and then select the user and double-click it.

The General Configuration Tab

General recipient configuration settings concern themselves with physical addresses and company information. As you can see in Figure 11.1, you have many available options:

- **First, Initials, Last, Display, Alias**—These fields contain the name of the user. The display name is what is shown to other users in the Address Book. The alias is a quick way to refer to this user.

- **Address, City, State, ZIP code, and Country**—These fields correlate to the physical address of the user. These fields are available to other users.

- **Title, Company, Department, and Office**—These fields relate to the user's company settings. The office field relates to the office or branch ID.

- **Assistant, Phone**—These fields are for the phone numbers of the user's assistant and the user.

- **Primary Windows NT Account**—The most important field on this screen, the Primary Windows NT Account correlates to the Windows NT server user account. This is an important setting for permissions.

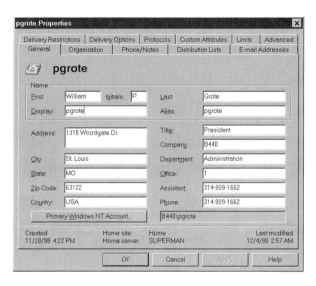

FIGURE **11.1**   The recipient General configuration tab.

You can access the **Properties** function under the Address Book and view all information under the General configuration tab (recipient), with the exception of the Windows NT Account information.

THE ORGANIZATION CONFIGURATION TAB

As shown in Figure 11.2, the Organization tab is responsible for one of the more powerful, but least-used functions of Microsoft Exchange 5.5. By entering the user's manager and direct reports information, Microsoft Exchange 5.5 will track your company's organizational chart.

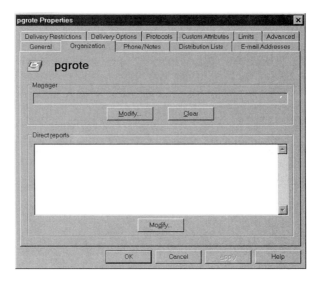

FIGURE 11.2   The recipient Organization configuration tab.

Choosing to implement the Organization feature of Microsoft Exchange 5.5 does have some ramifications for future administration. When employees change departments or change managers, modifications will need to be made.

Organization information is available for viewing by all users by selecting the **Properties** function in the Address Book.

THE PHONE/NOTES CONFIGURATION TAB

As shown in Figure 11.3, the Phones/Notes tab is comprehensive. You can include the following phone numbers:

- **Business**—The recipient's business phone number.

- **Business 2**—The recipient's alternative business phone number.

- **Fax**—The recipient's fax number.

- **Assistant**—The recipient's assistant's phone number.

- **Home**—The recipient's home phone number.

- **Home 2**—The recipient's alternative home phone number.

- **Mobile**—The recipient's cellular or digital phone number.

- **Pager**—The recipient's pager number.

FIGURE **11.3** The recipient Phones/Notes configuration tab.

As you can see, the list of phone numbers is very complete. Each of the phone numbers is available to other users by looking at the Properties of the recipient in the Address Book.

In the Notes section of the screen, you can comment on any aspect of the recipient. Common notes left here would detail any moves or changes to the account, the last trouble call, or any special requirements for the recipient.

 Viewing Restrictions   Notes left concerning a recipient are viewable only by administrators and not by users browsing the Global Address List.

THE DISTRIBUTION LISTS CONFIGURATION TAB

The Distribution Lists tab, shown in Figure 11.4, shows which Distribution Lists the recipient is a member of.

You can alter the Distribution Lists membership by clicking the **Modify** button.

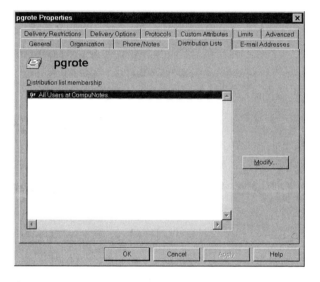

FIGURE 11.4   The recipient Distribution Lists configuration tab.

Distribution Lists' information is available for viewing by other users using the **Properties** function of the Address Book.

THE EMAIL ADDRESSES CONFIGURATION TAB

As you can see in Figure 11.5, the E-Mail Addresses tab shows each of the valid email addresses for the recipient.

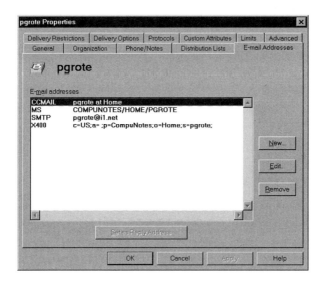

FIGURE **11.5** The recipient E-Mail Addresses configuration tab.

The recipient will have a different email address for each connector you have installed on the server.

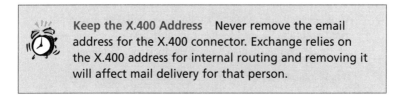

Keep the X.400 Address Never remove the email address for the X.400 connector. Exchange relies on the X.400 address for internal routing and removing it will affect mail delivery for that person.

The email addresses information is available for viewing by other users. Click the **Properties** function of the Address Book.

THE DELIVERY RESTRICTIONS CONFIGURATION TAB

The Delivery Restrictions tab, shown in Figure 11.6, shows any restrictions placed on this recipient for receiving email messages.

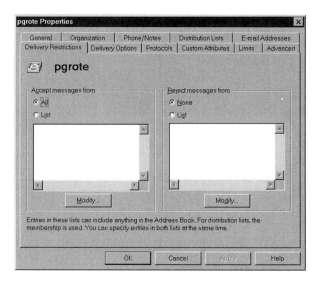

FIGURE 11.6   The Delivery Restrictions configuration tab.

You can configure restrictions based on two factors:

1. **Accept Messages**—You can restrict which messages this recipient accepts. There are two settings: All (the default) and List. If **All** is selected, all messages are delivered, unless the sender is specified in the Reject Messages field. If **List** is selected, you can specify certain senders who can email this recipient.

   This is a great feature for protecting beeper recipients. By accepting messages from only those users who have access, you can limit the number of non-critical pages.

2. **Reject Messages**—You can restrict which messages this recipient will reject. There are two settings: None (the default) and List. If **None** is selected, all messages are accepted. If **List** is selected, you can specify certain senders whose messages will be denied.

   You can use this feature to ensure certain users do not receive All Users messages. This is a useful feature if you employ temporary workers.

THE DELIVERY OPTIONS CONFIGURATION TAB

The Delivery Options tab, shown in Figure 11.7, displays who has permissions to send and receive messages in this recipient's name.

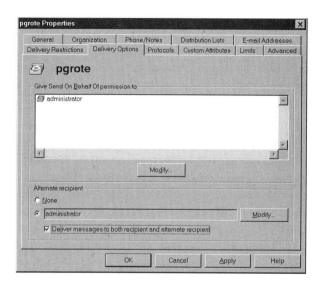

FIGURE 11.7   The recipient Delivery Options configuration tab.

You can change the permissions granted to other users for this recipient by clicking the **Modify** button. You also can grant multiple users permission to send email in the recipient's name, but only one user can be assigned as an alternative recipient.

There's an Alternative   If an alternative recipient is chosen, all email destined for the recipient is forwarded to the alternative recipient. Sometimes you might need to have a copy of all emails go to the original recipient and the alternative recipient. If this is the case, make sure you change the Deliver Messages field to the Both Recipient and Alternate Recipient option.

The Delivery Options feature is excellent for two purposes:

1. **Upper Management**—Many upper-management staff in corporate settings want to route all their email through their secretary. This is especially important for shared calendars.

2. **Multiple Email Aliases**—Sometimes it is necessary to add a special email address to a system that has the sole purpose of forwarding email to one user. For instance, an employee mascot might have an email address for employee children to send a message to. The messages sent to this email address can be automatically forwarded to one alternative recipient.

THE PROTOCOLS CONFIGURATION TAB

As you can see in Figure 11.8, the Protocols tab shows controls permissions to the various protocols used to deliver Microsoft Exchange 5.5 email.

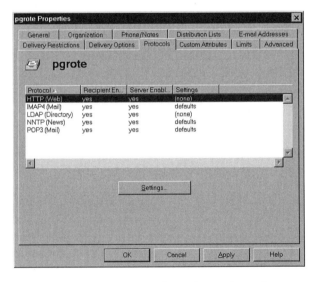

FIGURE **11.8**   The recipient Protocols configuration tab.

Microsoft Exchange 5.5 allows for the use of multiple client protocols. For instance, you can use HTTP via Outlook Web Access or POP3 from almost any Internet email client. You can enable and disable permissions to these protocols.

Permissions aren't the only configuration options. When using the **Settings** command on IMAP4 and POP3, you can control settings such as file attachments and message retrieval.

Denying certain recipients access to some protocols is a good method of improving Microsoft Exchange 5.5 security.

THE CUSTOM ATTRIBUTES CONFIGURATION TAB

The Custom Attributes tab, shown in Figure 11.9, displays the data for user-defined fields.

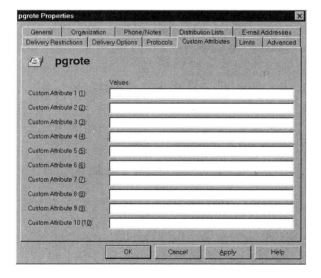

FIGURE 11.9   The recipient Custom Attributes configuration tab.

Microsoft Exchange 5.5 is extremely configurable. Sometimes you might want to note information on recipients that isn't available under Microsoft Exchange 5.5.

To solve this problem, Microsoft Exchange 5.5 allows you to define and propagate 10 extra fields for each recipient. These data fields can contain any type of data you define.

Some common uses for the custom attributes are as follows:

* Social Security Number

* Employee ID Number

* Hire date

* Spouse name

* Birth date

* Parking space allocation

* Shift number

* Car license plate number

* Hard-coded TCP/IP address

The Custom Attribute fields are not accessible to users through the Address Book.

THE LIMITS CONFIGURATION TAB

As shown in Figure 11.10, the Limits tab allows the Microsoft Exchange 5.5 administrator to limit many mail settings for the recipient.

The following mail settings can be limited:

* **Deleted Item Retention Time**—Typically you would want to use the Information Store default setting, but you can set the number of days mail objects exist before being deleted. The option **Don't Permanently Delete Items Until the Store has Been Backed Up** should be enabled as a safety net.

* **Information Store Limits**—Again, you would probably want to use the Information Store default setting, but you can override

these settings. You can set the amount of storage space in kilobytes that must be reached before a warning is issued, and mail will be prohibited from being sent and received.

- **Message Size Outgoing**—You can limit the size of outgoing mail messages in kilobytes. The default setting is **No Limit**.

- **Message Size Incoming**—You can limit the size of incoming mail messages in kilobytes. The default setting is **No Limit**.

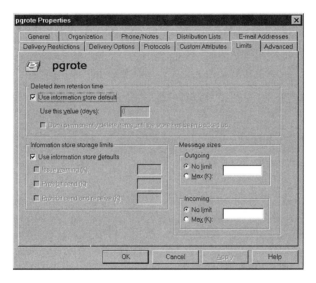

FIGURE 11.10   The recipient Limits configuration tab.

Setting mail limits for a specific recipient should only be done as a last resort. The Information Store settings should be the default values for each user.

THE ADVANCED CONFIGURATION TAB

The Advanced tab, shown in Figure 11.11, allows the Microsoft Exchange 5.5 administrator to restrict many settings for the recipient.

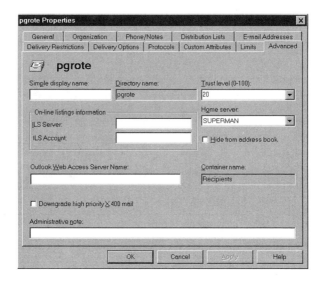

FIGURE 11.11   The recipient Advanced configuration tab.

The following settings can be limited:

- **Simple Display Name**—This command is used to ensure the recipient's ID can be used by foreign email systems. Sometimes special characters do not have similar characters on other systems. The Simple Display Name offers you a field to ensure only alphabetical or numeric characters are used.

- **Trust Level**—Internal to Microsoft Exchange 5.5 is the trust level. A trust level is used by Directory Replication to decide if an object should be replicated to another container. If a recipient object's trust level is higher than the destination container, the recipient object is not replicated.

- **ILS Server**—The Internet Locator Service is used to coordinate NetMeeting online meetings. This field contains the ILS server name to use.

- **ILS Account**—Again, the Internet Locator Service is used to coordinate NetMeeting online meetings. This field contains the ILS account name to use.

- **Home Server**—This field indicates the user's home server. You can move users from one server to another in the same site by using the **Move Mailbox** tool in Exchange Administrator.

- **Hide from Address Book**—Enable this setting if you would like this recipient hidden in the Address Book. You could use this feature to ensure a person, such as the president of the company, is not listed in the Address Book.

- **Outlook Web Access Server Name**—Typically you would want to use the Information Store default setting, but if you need to change this setting you can.

- **Downgrade High Priority X.400 Mail**—High priority mail will be downgraded to normal mail if this setting is active.

- **Administrative Note**—You can enter up to 1,024 characters. A note on why certain restrictions or changes were made is a good use of this field.

SHORTCUTS: A TIMESAVING TIP FOR THE EXCHANGE ADMINISTRATOR

Microsoft Exchange 5.5's recipient configuration is comprehensive. But what happens if you need to add a new user? Trying to make sure all the configuration information is the same for each user you create is a long and tedious process.

Luckily, Microsoft included the **Duplicate** command. Select the recipient object that contains the configuration information you would like to pass on to a new user. For example, you could create one recipient having all the settings for your account executives, and duplicate this master as necessary when new employees arrive.

Next, select **File, Duplicate**. Notice that a new recipient object is created in a dialog box. The only fields you need to propagate are First, Initial, Last, Display, and Alias.

Make sure you name your template account something similar to the template because you might have multiple templates, depending on your installation.

In this lesson you learned how to use the Microsoft Administrator program to define and configure various aspects for each user.

LESSON 12

CREATING AND USING PUBLIC FOLDERS

In this lesson you'll learn how to use and configure public folders.

PUBLIC FOLDERS EXPLAINED

Public folders are a new idea to email systems. In a typical email system, messages are sent from user to user. If a user wants to share a message with the rest of the organization, they would have to forward that message to each user. With Microsoft Exchange 5.5, however, you can use public folders to share information with the organization by depositing a single copy of a message in a location everyone has access to. The function is analogous to a public bulletin board.

Public folders are similar to private folders you create in your mailbox, but they are available to everyone in the organization.

You can control access to public folders through *Access Controls Lists* (ACLs). Each Public Folder can have its own ACL, in which specific users or distribution lists can be granted or denied access.

 Access Control Lists ACLs are similar to the ACLS's found on files and directory throughout the Windows NT file system because they control what permissions a user or distribution list has to a certain resource.

WHAT CAN BE PUT IN A PUBLIC FOLDER?

Any information type you can store in your personal folders can be stored in public folders. These include the following:

- **Mail Messages**—A public folder can be a recipient of an email message just like any other user. This is a good idea for sharing non-critical information with the entire organization.

 Distribute Mail to Public Folders Public Folders can be members of a Distribution List. This is a good feature for keeping archived copies of committee messages, etc.

- **Documents**—Files created by applications such as Microsoft Word, Microsoft Excel, and so on, can be copied to public folders. You can drag and drop documents into the public folder. This is a good way of making sure the company phone extension list or vacation policy is up to date.

- **Graphic Files**—Microsoft PowerPoint presentations and other graphic files can be copied to public folders. You can drag and drop graphic files into the public folder.

- **Files**—Miscellaneous files such as data files can be copied to the public folders. Again, you can drag and drop the files into the public folder.

- **Exchange Forms**—Exchange Forms can be placed in a public folder so an entire organization can use them. This is perfect for feedback or survey forms. You'll learn more about creating and using forms in Lesson 18, "Microsoft Exchange 5.5 Forms."

- **Internet Newsgroups**—Internet newsgroups can be added to the public folder hierarchy, giving users complete access to the Internet newsgroups.

How Does that Information Get Into Public Folders?

Users can submit information to a public folder in many ways including the following:

- **Posting items to a public folder**—Creating an item in a public folder is accomplished just as you would create a mail message. You can add any information, including files and documents.

- **Addressing items to a public folder**—Public folders display as an addressee in the Global Address List (GAL). This makes it easy for a user to CC: the list to share information. You can also use this feature to store a record of announcements or broadcast messages.

 Make Public Folders Globally Accessible   Public Folders do not appear in the GAL by default. You must disable the **Hide From Address Book** option under the Object configuration screen for the public folder.

- **Users can drag and drop information to a public folder**—This features works out great for users who want to share common programming code or HTML designs.

Figure 12.1 shows a public folder called Employee News. Notice that the first two items in the folder are direct posts to the folder. The third item is a mail message addressed to the public folder. The last two items were dragged on to the public folder.

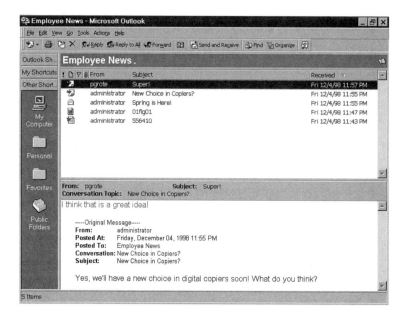

FIGURE 12.1   A public folder with several objects.

PUBLIC FOLDER ADMINISTRATION

Up to this point, Microsoft has done a good job of bringing public folders to an organization. The administration of public folders is a simple concept to understand, but in practice it can seem a little more difficult.

CREATING A PUBLIC FOLDER

The first hurdle you need to overcome is understanding that creation and deletion of public folders is handled through the client. Even though this feature of Microsoft Exchange 5.5 is for organizational communication, public folders are born and die with the client.

To create a public folder, complete the following steps:

1. Open **Outlook 98** and select **Public Folders** from the **Other Shortcuts** menu.

2. Open the **All Public Folders** folder.

3. Select the **File** menu, choose **Folders**, select **New Folder**, and then enter the name of the new folder, as shown in Figure 12.2.

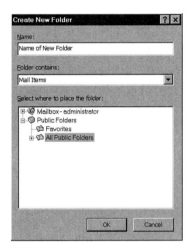

FIGURE 12.2   Creating a public folder.

 Outlook 98 Folders Are Versatile   When you use Outlook 98 to create a new public folder, you are not limited to mail folders. You can create Contact, Calendar, Task, Journal, and Note folders.

RESTRICTING ACCESS TO CREATE PUBLIC FOLDERS

Giving the ability to create public folders to the clients might empower users, but your organization might not want all users to have this power.

Fortunately, you can restrict who can create public folders by modifying the Information Store Site configuration object. The following steps will enable you to control access:

1. Select the site where you would like to restrict public folder creation.

2. Select the **Configuration** object.

3. Select the **Information Store Site Configuration** object.

4. Select the **Top Level Folder Creation** tab.

5. Modify the access lists as shown in Figure 12.3.

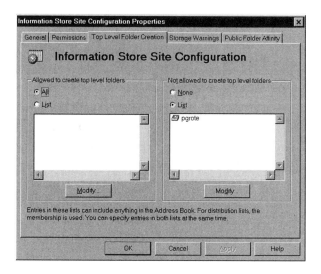

FIGURE 12.3   Restricting access for creating public folders.

DELETING PUBLIC FOLDERS

Deleting a public folder is also a simple process. To do so, follow these steps:

1. Launch **Outlook 98** if necessary and select **Public Folders** from the **Other Shortcuts** menu.

2. Highlight the public folder you want to delete.

3. Select the **File** menu, choose **Folders, Delete Folder**, and then select **Yes**, as shown in Figure 12.4.

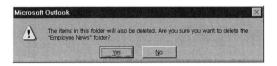

FIGURE 12.4   Deleting a public folder.

PUBLIC FOLDER PROPERTIES

Even though the client handles the creation and deletion of the public folder, the Exchange administrator has full server-side control including setting public folder properties.

PUBLIC FOLDER PROPERTIES

Each public folder can be configured through the Properties screen. In Exchange Administrator, click **Folders**, select **Public Folders**, and highlight the folder you created previously. Click on the **File** menu and select **Properties**. You will see the areas of configuration listed here:

- General

- Replicas

- Folder Replication status

- Replication schedule

- Distribution lists

- Email addresses

- Custom attributes

- Limits

- Advanced

THE GENERAL CONFIGURATION TAB

Under the General configuration tab, there are five configuration aspects you can control, as shown in Figure 12.5.

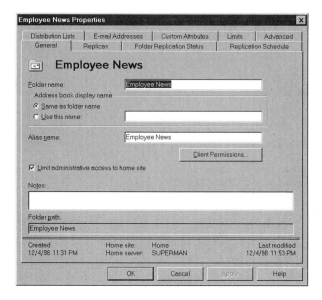

FIGURE 12.5   The General configuration tab for public folder properties.

- **Address book display name**—The default value for this option is the actual name of the public folder. You can change this to a more friendly or descriptive name if you want.

- **Alias name**—You can enter an alias name for the public folder. This makes it easier to address messages to the public folder in the To field. For instance, the Global Warming Treaty Fiasco folder could have an alias of GWTF. This would allow users to address their messages to GWTF instead of the entire name.

- **Client permissions**—You can control access to the public folder by clicking this button. The default permissions for a public folder are inherited from the Information Store Site configuration.

There are predefined permission settings for certain users. The predefined settings are Contributor, Reviewer, Non-Editing Author, Author, Publishing Author, Editor, Publishing Editor, Owner, and Custom.

Predefined role settings have the capabilities, as shown in Table 12.1.

TABLE 12.1   PREDEFINED ROLES

PREDEFINED ROLE	PERMISSIONS
Owner	Create Items, Read Items, Create Subfolders, Folder Owner, Folder Contact, Edit All, Delete All, Folder Visible
Publishing Editor	Create Items, Read Items, Create Subfolders, Edit All, Delete All, Folder Visible
Editor	Create Items, Read Items, Edit All, Delete All, Folder Visible
Publishing Author	Create Items, Read Items, Create Subfolders, Edit Own, Delete Own, Folder Visible
Author	Create Items, Read Items, Edit Own, Delete Own, Folder Visible
Non-editing Author	Create Items, Read Items, Delete Own, Folder Visible
Reviewer	Read Items, Folder Visible
Contributor	Create Items, Read Items, Folder Visible

- **Limit administrative access to home site**—Enable this option if you would like to ensure administration of public folders to the installed site.

- **Notes**—You can keep notes on public folders. This is a handy feature for noting ownership changes and the purpose of the public folder.

THE REPLICAS CONFIGURATION TAB

The Replicas configuration tab controls which other Microsoft Exchange 5.5 servers contain local copies of the public folder. The control process is shown in the dialog box in Figure 12.6.

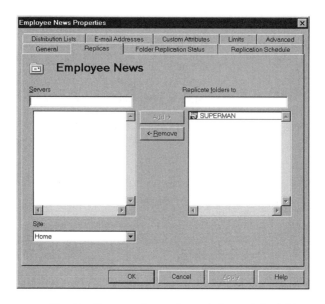

FIGURE 12.6   The Replicas configuration tab for public folder properties.

A *replica* is a copy of an object. Public folders can have replicas that are copied to other servers. This is a great way to share information with other sites.

To add a server to the replica configuration, click on the server you want to replicate, and then click **OK**. You can remove a server by clicking on the server, and then clicking **Delete**.

The advantages of public folder replication include

- **Fault Tolerance**—Copies of your public folder will be on multiple servers. If one fails, you won't lose any information.

- **Load Balancing**—Instead of having one server handling the traffic to one public folder, you can have multiple servers involved.

- **Traffic Reduction**—WAN traffic to your servers will be disbursed when the public folder is replicated.

THE FOLDER REPLICATION STATUS CONFIGURATION TAB

The Folder Replication Status configuration tab displays a log of the current replication processes. The log is shown in Figure 12.7.

FIGURE 12.7   The Folder Replication Status configuration tab for public folder properties.

The log details the server name you are replicating to, the time data was last received, the average transmission time, and the current replication status. This is an excellent tool for troubleshooting.

THE REPLICATION SCHEDULE CONFIGURATION TAB

The Replication Schedule configuration tab allows you to set a schedule for periodic replication, as shown in Figure 12.8.

The Replication Schedule allows you to specify when public folders are replicated. The default value is to use the Information Store schedule. You can also elect to turn off replication.

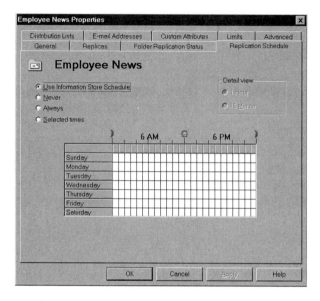

FIGURE 12.8   The Replication Schedule configuration tab for public folder properties.

THE DISTRIBUTION LISTS CONFIGURATION TAB

The Distribution Lists configuration tab allows you to add the public folder to a Distribution List, as shown in Figure 12.9.

Public Folders are objects just like recipients. As such, you can add a public folder to a distribution list. When you do this, any message sent to the distribution list will be distributed to the public folder as well as the individuals.

You also can directly modify the membership of the distribution lists from this screen. To do so, double-click on the distribution list name.

THE E-MAIL ADDRESSES CONFIGURATION TAB

The E-Mail Addresses configuration tab displays the email address of the public folder for each connector, as shown in Figure 12.10.

FIGURE **12.9**   The Distribution Lists Configuration Tab for public folder Properties.

FIGURE **12.10**   The E-Mail Addresses configuration tab for public folder properties.

Other email clients on foreign email systems that send messages to the
public folder can use these email addresses.

THE CUSTOM ATTRIBUTES CONFIGURATION TAB

The Custom Attributes configuration tab allows you to propagate up to 10
fields of data, as shown in Figure 12.11.

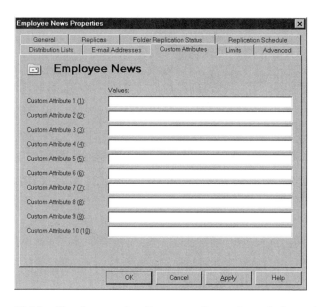

FIGURE **12.11**   The Custom Attributes configuration tab for public
folder properties.

Because public folders are objects like recipients, you can assign values
to custom attributes.

THE LIMITS CONFIGURATION TAB

The Limits configuration tab allows you to limit the storage space and age
of items in the public folder. You can also limit how long deleted items
are stored.

Limiting storage space might be necessary if your Microsoft Exchange
Server 5.5 has limited resources.

Microsoft Exchange 5.5's public folder features a maintenance-free administration procedure and offers the capability to save deleted items. You will never have to clean up the deleted files, as Microsoft Exchange 5.5 deletes them for you.

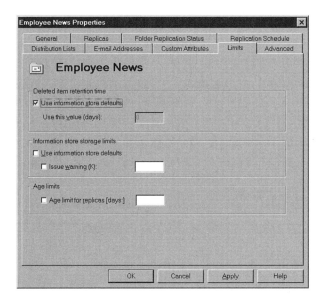

FIGURE **12.12**   The Limits configuration tab for public folder properties.

Edit Restrictions or Receive Defaults   If you don't set limits for the public folder, Microsoft Exchange 5.5 will use the Information Store default settings.

THE ADVANCED CONFIGURATION TAB

There are five fields you can modify for the Advanced configuration tab:

- **Simple Display Name**—This command is used to ensure the public folder's ID can be used by foreign email systems. Sometimes special characters do not have similar characters on other systems. The simple display name offers you a field to ensure only alphanumeric characters are used.

- **Replicating Message Importance**—You can select a priority level that affects the order in which Microsoft Exchange 5.5 sends messages. Messages with high priority are delivered first.

- **Trust Level**—Internal to Microsoft Exchange 5.5 is the trust level. A trust level is used by Directory Replication to decide if an object should be replicated to another container. If a public folder's trust level is higher than the destination container, the public folder is not replicated.

- **Hide From Address Book**—By default, this option is enabled when a public folder is created. Disabling this feature allows the public folder to appear in the Address Book.

- **Administrative Note**—You have up to 1,024 characters to describe any advanced features of the public folder. You might want to note the last time a modification was made to the trust level.

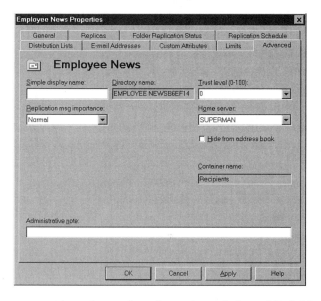

FIGURE 12.13   The Advanced configuration tab for public folder properties.

INTERSITE PUBLIC FOLDER ACCESS

With users creating public folders on their Microsoft Exchange 5.5 servers, you might find that not everyone who needs access to a particular public folder is located in the same site. Microsoft Exchange 5.5 handles access to intersite public folders through public folder *Affinity*.

At first you may think Affinity is an odd choice to describe access settings for a public folder. At the very least it is as low tech as low tech gets. Affinity typically means a kinship and in the case of public folders this is true as well.

Affinity not only allows you to grant intersite access to public folders, but it also allows you to specify the order in which access will be attempted. By setting the Affinity value, you can offer redundancy and fault tolerance for your public folders.

For example, you have three sites, Site1, Site2, and Site3. Site1 contains the original public folders. Replicas of the public folders exist on Site2 and Site3. You can force intersite users to access the public folders on Site3 by setting the Affinity value of Site3 lower than Site2. Microsoft Exchange 5.5 will attempt to access the public folders based on the lowest Affinity value.

INTERSITE PUBLIC FOLDER ACCESS

So, just how do you set up the public folder Affinity relationship and value? Of course, you'll need Microsoft Exchange Administrator!

Open Microsoft Exchange Administrator to the originating site of the public folders you want to grant access to. Select the Information Store Site Configuration object from the Configuration container. Click on the **Public Folder Affinity** tab and a screen similar to Figure 12.14 will appear.

In Figure 12.14, you are changing the Public Folder Affinity for site B440. You've granted access to the Home site with an Affinity value of 1. This means that all users in the Home site can now access public folders on the B440 site.

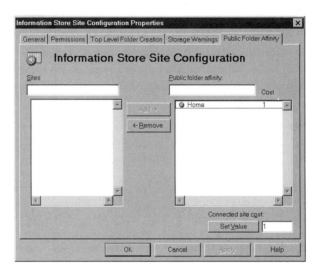

FIGURE 12.14 Creating a Public Folder Affinity setting.

 Network Connectivity Needed Public folder Affinities can only be created between sites with network connectivity that support RPC (Remote Procedure Call).

Way to go! Public folders are certainly one of the most difficult concepts to fully understand in Microsoft Exchange 5.5.

In this lesson, you learned how to create and configure public folders. Additionally, you learned how to grant other sites access to your public folders.

LESSON 13
DIRECTORY REPLICATION

In this lesson you'll learn the concept and purpose of Directory Replication.

Directory Replication makes your life as a Microsoft Exchange 5.5 administrator much easier. Through copying directory information from one server to another, the entire organization has access to the information without human intervention.

TYPES OF DIRECTORY REPLICATION

There are two types of Directory Replication depending on your organization's configuration:

1. **Intrasite**—Directory Replication occurs among servers within the same site.

2. **Intersite**—Directory Replication occurs among servers with different sites.

INTRASITE DIRECTORY REPLICATION

If your organization has a single site or is not connected to another site, you don't need to do anything to enable Directory Replication.

Directory Replication for an intrasite installation is handled via Remote Procedure Calls (RPCs). You don't need to have a formal connector installed.

During installation of a new Microsoft Exchange Server 5.5 in your site, you need to ensure your *service account* is configured properly and the correct password is specified. This process is covered in Lesson 5, "Installing Microsoft Exchange."

Service Account   An administrative account used by Microsoft Exchange 5.5 to perform system functions.

If you do try to install a Directory Replication container on a single site system, you will receive an error message similar to the one shown in Figure 13.1.

FIGURE 13.1   Installing a Directory Replication container in a single site installation.

INTERSITE DIRECTORY REPLICATION

When Directory Replication occurs between two sites, you use a direct connection. Replicating three or more sites requires the use of a *Bridgehead server.*

Bridgehead Server   A Bridgehead server is the *gateway* or main server used to collect messages from one site for transferring to another site. Think of the Bridgehead server as an airport—all the people (messages) travel to the airport (Bridgehead server) to be flown (transferred) to another city (site).

A Bridgehead server handles the Directory Replication processes for each site. Even though there might be 10 servers in one site, only one server actually handles Directory Replication, as shown in Figure 13.2.

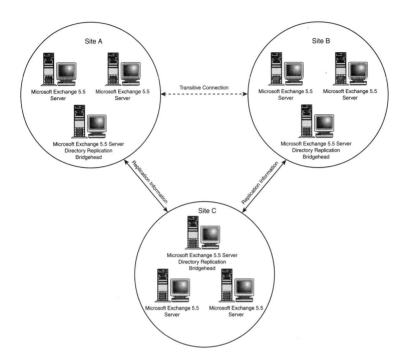

FIGURE 13.2   Bridgehead servers are required for more than three sites.

 Replication Requires a Single Path   Sites cannot have two Directory Replication paths to a remote site. They can have connectors between them, but the Directory Replication connection is termed a< transitive connection.

When changes are made to the directory in a site, Exchange sends a message to the Directory Replication Bridgehead server. The Bridgehead server receives the message, and then responds with a request for the information. The information is then compiled and sent to other sites when the Directory Replication schedule permits.

CREATING A DIRECTORY REPLICATION CONNECTOR

When you are creating a Directory Replication connector, you need to know the service account information for your site and the remote site. After you have this information, execute Exchange Administrator by performing the following steps:

1. Click the **Start** menu.

2. Choose **Programs**.

3. Select the **Microsoft Exchange** group.

4. Launch the **Microsoft Exchange Administrator**.

After Exchange Administrator is loaded, select the Directory Replication container under the Site Configuration container, as shown in Figure 13.3.

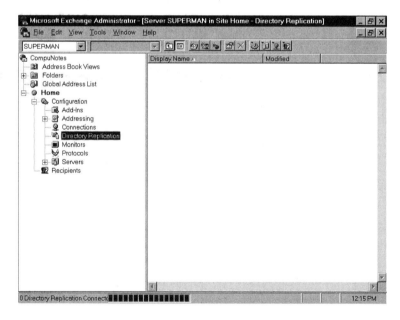

FIGURE 13.3   Selecting the Directory Replication container.

After you highlight the Directory Replication container, follow these steps as shown in Figure 13.4.

1. Select the **File** menu.

2. Choose **New Other**.

3. Select **Directory Replication Connector**.

FIGURE **13.4**   The new Directory Replication connector command.

A configuration dialog box will appear, as shown in Figure 13.5. You will need to complete the requested information.

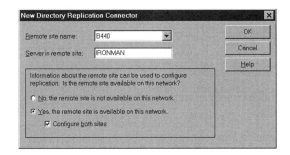

FIGURE **13.5**   The New Directory Replication Connector configuration screen.

You can edit the following fields:

- **Remote site name**—This is the site name that is not yours.

- **Server in remote site**—This is the specific server that exists in the other site.

- **Server availability**—There are two options. You can select the server to be available on the local network or not. If it is on the local network, you can configure both sides concurrently.

When you click **OK**, you'll be presented with the General tab of the Directory Replication connector object's Properties dialog box. Figure 13.6 shows the configuration options.

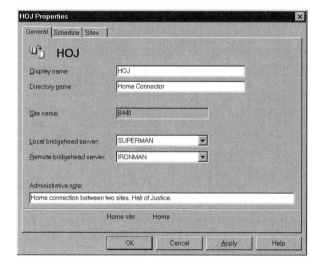

FIGURE **13.6**   The General tab for Directory Replication connector properties.

You can configure the following settings:

- **Display name**—The display name shows in the Exchange Administrator window.

- **Directory name**—The directory name is used for internal Microsoft Exchange 5.5 communications. You can use the same name as the display name.

- **Local Bridgehead server**—This is the Microsoft Exchange 5.5
  Server on your site that you will use as a Bridgehead server.

- **Remote Bridgehead server**—This is the Microsoft Exchange
  5.5 Server on the remote site used as a Bridgehead server.

- **Administrative note**—You can append a note of up to 1,024
  characters to describe the connection.

The next tab under Directory Replication properties is Schedule. As you
can see in Figure 13.7, the Schedule in this example is configured to
update Directory Replication modifications every three hours. You can
choose to **Never** distribute modifications, **Always** distribute modifications
as they arrive, or modify the default schedule.

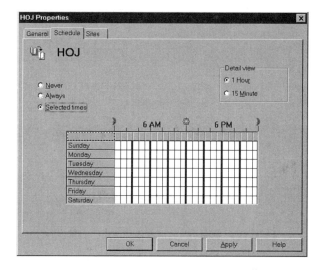

FIGURE **13.7**   The Schedule tab for Directory Replication connector
properties.

The final tab is Sites. The Sites tab shows what servers are participating
in Directory Replication and whether they are inbound or outbound sites.

Inbound sites send updates to the Bridgehead server, and outbound sites
receive the updates from the Bridgehead server.

As shown in Figure 13.8, the most important function of this tab is the Request Now button. If critical directory information isn't being propagated due to scheduling issues, you can click **Request Now** to begin the process. This action overrides the default schedule.

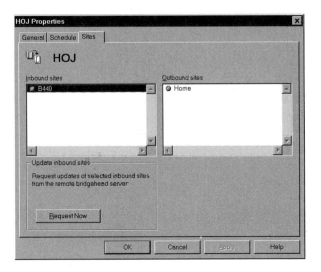

FIGURE **13.8**   The Sites tab for Directory Replication connector properties.

 Be Sure to Restart   Changes to the Directory Replication configuration don't take effect until the Directory Service on the local and remote server is restarted.

In this lesson you learned the purpose of Directory Replication and how to implement it.

LESSON 14

BACKUP AND RESTORE PLANNING AND TESTING

In this lesson, you'll learn what types of data you should back up when you're using Microsoft Exchange 5.5, such as transaction logs and the Registry; what types of backups are available; and how to use the NTBACKUP program.

Microsoft Exchange 5.5 is essentially one large database—one large database that never sleeps, so to speak. While the Microsoft Exchange services are running, the database data is continually changing. There is no point in time where a single snapshot of the database can be made. As with any database, there must be a way to back up the data without having to stop the Exchange services. This is called an *online backup*.

WHAT NEEDS TO BE BACKED UP?

The first question that must be answered is which elements you need to back up. Microsoft Exchange 5.5 is comprised of several databases. You will want to back up the items in the following list, but among these, transaction logs, program files, and the Registry are the most important to back up.

- Microsoft Exchange 5.5 databases and other production files

- Transaction logs

- Windows NT and Microsoft Exchange 5.5 system files

- The Registry

MICROSOFT EXCHANGE 5.5 DATABASES

Microsoft Exchange 5.5 uses subdirectories to delineate database struc-
tures. Table 14.1 indicates which databases are stored in the subdirectories
of the \EXCHSRVR directory.

TABLE 14.1   DATABASE STORAGE LOCATIONS

SUBDIRECTORY	DATABASE OR PRODUCTION FILES
DSADATA	Directory Service—DIR.EDB
MDBDATA	Private Information Store—PRIV.EDB
	Public Information Store—PUB.EDU
KMSDATA	Key Management
MTADATA	Mail Transfer Agent
TRACKING.LOG	Logging for Message Archival
DXADATA	MSMail Directory Synchronization
IMCDATA	Internet Mail Service

Figure 14.1 shows the native order of the subdirectories as they are
installed.

Each of these components is critical to Microsoft Exchange 5.5 and
should be backed up nightly.

Back Up Critical Components Nightly   At the risk of
repeating myself, I can't stress enough how important
it is to back up critical components such as the directory structure nightly.

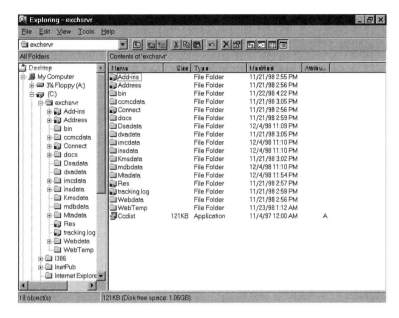

FIGURE 14.1   The native Microsoft Exchange 5.5 directory structure.

TRANSACTION LOGS

When a mail message is submitted to a Microsoft Exchange 5.5 Server, the Information Store databases are not modified at that moment. Instead the database commands that change the database are stored in a transaction log. After a period of time, the commands in the transaction log are flushed, and the data is committed to the Information Store. This feature is called *transaction logging*. Figure 14.2 shows the message flow for Microsoft Exchange 5.5 Server.

Transaction Logging Imagine being able to undo something you have done in your life. Better yet, how about being able to hand someone a recording of what you did during the day so they can do the same thing the next day? That's the essence of transaction logging. Microsoft Exchange 5.5 uses a transaction log to record each change to the Microsoft Exchange 5.5 databases. In the case of a mail failure, you can rest assured that your database will be recoverable because Microsoft Exchange 5.5 tracked all of its changes.

Here's the sequence transaction logging takes.

1. Outlook 98 (or another client) creates a new mail message and submits it to the Microsoft Exchange 5.5 Server.

2. The Microsoft Exchange 5.5 Server receives the message.

3. The Microsoft Exchange 5.5 Server processes the change to the Information Store in memory.

4. The Microsoft Exchange 5.5 Server then stores the modifications to the Information Store in a transaction log.

5. After a certain interval of time, the modification is read from the transaction log and committed to the Information Store.

If you back up your server and exclude backing up the transaction logs, changes that were made to your databases but not committed will be lost. You will not only lose data, but database consistency will be threatened as well.

Transaction Logs Are Vital Your backup routine must contain the transaction logs not just your server files. Otherwise, you're sure to lose data in the event of a failure.

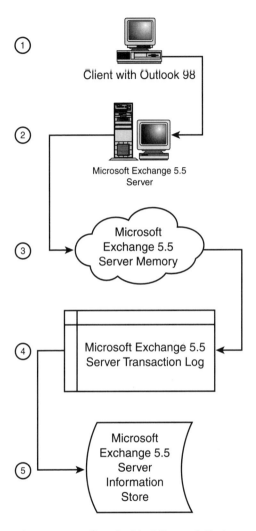

FIGURE **14.2**   The message flow inside Microsoft Exchange 5.5.

 File Size Is a Clue   One of the neat things about Microsoft Exchange 5.5 transaction logs is their size. They are typically around 5MB. If your log files are not this size, you should investigate possible corruption.

Database Committing   When an update or change is made to the Microsoft Exchange 5.5 database it is called database commitment. This means the change has actually been made to the Microsoft Exchange 5.5 database.

Log files have an extension of LOG unless more than one log file is needed for an extremely busy Microsoft Exchange 5.5 Server. If this is the case, the original log file, EDB.LOG, would be renamed EDB001.LOG.

As you can guess, pretty soon your Microsoft Exchange 5.5 Server would accumulate many log files. Microsoft decided to ship Microsoft Exchange 5.5 Server with a feature called *circular logging*. Circular logging manages the amount of log files by overwriting old log files. Sure, this scheme saves space, but it's an invitation for information loss in case of a restore. Information can be lost during a backup very easily. If your backup program has finished backing up the Microsoft Exchange 5.5 log files, but circular logging has written more information to the log files, you will lose that information. Worse yet, you might even corrupt the database on a restore.

If you disable circular logging, all Microsoft Exchange 5.5 log files are stored. If you do need to restore your Microsoft Exchange 5.5 Server in the future, you will suffer no data loss at all due to the fact that all the log files since the last backup have been kept. You might have already guessed that I recommend this method.

You can disable circular logging by using Exchange Administrator to select the Server object under the Configuration/Servers container, as shown in Figure 14.3.

After you have selected the server on that you would like to disable circular logging on, select the **File** menu and choose **Properties**, as shown in Figure 14.4.

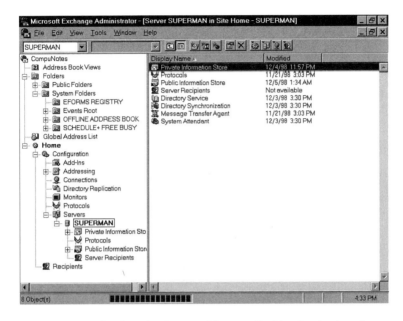

FIGURE 14.3   Selecting the Server object to disable circular logging.

FIGURE 14.4   Selecting server properties in Microsoft Exchange 5.5.

From the Properties screen select the **Advanced** tab and you will notice the options in Figure 14.5.

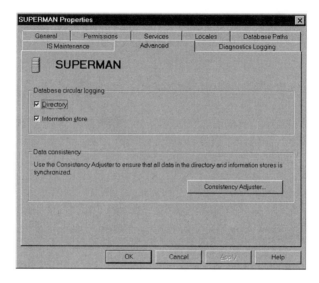

FIGURE 14.5   Selecting advanced server properties in Microsoft Exchange 5.5.

Disable the **Database circular logging** for both the Directory and Information Store. Select **OK**, and Microsoft Exchange 5.5 will warn you that Microsoft Exchange 5.5 will restart services needed for logging. Figure 14.6 shows the warning dialog box. Click **OK**.

FIGURE 14.6   Accepting the choice to disable circular logging.

When you click **OK** to acknowledge the warning box, Microsoft Exchange begins stopping then restarting the appropriate services, as shown in Figure 14.7.

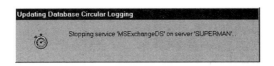

Figure 14.7   Stopping and restarting Microsoft Exchange 5.5 services.

Congratulations! Your Microsoft Exchange 5.5 Server is now fully prepared to crash. Seriously, if you are faithful and do backups daily, you can recover more quickly and more reliably now that circular logging is disabled.

WINDOWS NT AND MICROSOFT EXCHANGE 5.5 SYSTEM FILES

Under most circumstances, you will need to reinstall Windows NT Server and Microsoft Exchange 5.5 prior to restoring. The question then becomes: Should you take the time and resources to back up the system files? The answer is a qualified yes. Ensure you are backing up at the very least the \EXCHSRVR and the \WINNT subdirectory trees.

THE REGISTRY

The Registry contains critical configuration information for your Microsoft Exchange 5.5 Server. You should ensure that your backup software always makes a backup of your Registry.

Most of the Microsoft Exchange 5.5-related information can be found at HKEY_LOCAL_MACHINE\SOFTWARE\Microsoft\Exchange or HKEY_LOCAL_MACHINE\SYSTEM\CurrentControlSet\Services.

HOW SHOULD YOU BACK UP THE DATA?

Microsoft Exchange 5.5 includes an updated NTBACKUP utility that supports the methods of backing up an Exchange installation. By default, when Exchange is installed, it replaces the NTBACKUP.EXE by the following process:

1. Click the **Start** menu.

2. Click **Programs**.

3. Choose **Administrative Tools (Common)**.

4. Select **Backup**.

Following these steps will reveal the backup program, as shown in Figure 14.8.

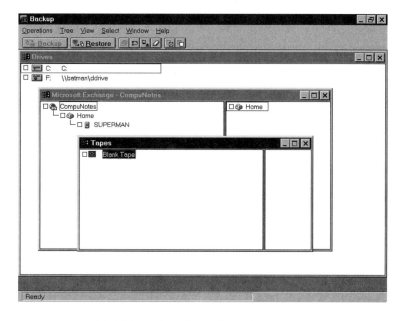

FIGURE 14.8   NTBACKUP, the Microsoft Backup program.

There are two types of backups supported by NTBACKUP.EXE:

- **Online Backups**—Data is backed up while services are running and the database is open.

- **Offline Backups**—Data is backed up with services stopped and the database closed.

ONLINE BACKUP

Exchange supports four types of online backups:

1. Normal/Full
2. Copy
3. Incremental
4. Differential

NORMAL/FULL BACKUPS

A normal/full backup backs up your database files first, and then your log files. After the backup is complete, the log files are deleted. If you're performing daily backups, you won't have to worry about log files taking up an unusual amount of hard drive space. The normal/full backup also resets the backup archive bit on the databases. Restoring a normal/full backup is as easy as restoring the last normal/full backup, and then restarting the services.

You should use normal/full backups on a daily basis.

COPY BACKUPS

A copy backup is similar to a normal/full backup except the copy backup doesn't delete log files or reset the archive bit.

A copy backup is a good choice if you are interested in doing a quick backup outside of your normal backup schedule.

 When to Perform Unscheduled Backups   Performing a backup outside your normal backup schedule is an especially good idea before installing new software or implementing another change in your Exchange system.

INCREMENTAL BACKUPS

Incremental backups back up the log files only. You can use this type of backup only when circular logging is disabled. Incremental backups delete the log files after the backup is complete.

You don't restore an incremental backup by itself, but you restore it after your normal/full backup is restored. You should restore the normal/full backup first, and then layer the subsequent incremental backups. When you are finished restoring the last incremental backup, the transaction logs are applied in order to the Exchange database that was restored with the normal/full backup.

Make Sure Your Incremental Backups Are Restored Do not restart the Microsoft Exchange 5.5 services until all the incremental backups have been restored. If you attempt to do this, you will lose data.

DIFFERENTIAL BACKUPS

Differential backups are similar to incremental backups in that they work with log files, but they don't delete the log files after a complete backup.

You don't restore a differential backup by itself, but you restore it after your normal/full backup is restored. You should restore the normal/full backup first, and then restore the differential backup.

Restore All Your Incremental Backups Before Restarting   Again, this point bears emphasizing: Do not restart the Microsoft Exchange 5.5 services until all the incremental backups have been restored. If you do this, you will lose data.

The time to complete an online backup obviously depends on the backup type you select. A normal/full backup will take the longest, followed by copy, incremental, and differential backups.

Which backup type should you choose? Table 14.2 lists the advantages and disadvantages of each type.

TABLE 14.2 ADVANTAGES AND DISADVANTAGES OF BACKUP TYPES

BACKUP TYPE	ADVANTAGE	DISADVANTAGE
Daily Normal/ Full Alone	Simplicity. Ease of restore. Manages log files.	Takes longer to backup larger Microsoft Exchange 5.5 installations. Tape swap might be necessary.
Copy Alone	Quick copy of current data.	Not the best restoration method. Might be missing data. Doesn't manage log files.
Weekly Normal/ Full with Daily Incremental	Minimum backup time. Fewer resources used than a normal/ full backup.	Restore can be complex requiring up to seven restores.
Weekly Normal/ Full with Daily Differential	Fewer resources used than a normal/ full backup. Multiple log file back ups.	Backup time increases each day. Restores require two restores.

OFFLINE BACKUP

The Offline backup backs up all Exchange files and databases while the Microsoft Exchange 5.5-related services are stopped on the server. It is a good idea once or twice a month to have an offline backup in case your online backups are corrupted for any reason.

Remember, offline backups do not manage the Microsoft Exchange 5.5 log files. You will have to delete the older log files manually.

You should never use offline backups as your primary backup type, unless you want to disable access to your Exchange server for a few hours each night while it gets backed up.

POTENTIAL BACKUP/RESTORE ISSUES

There are two potential issues you should consider when planning a backup strategy for Microsoft Exchange 5.5:

1. Key Management
2. Windows NT Registry

KEY MANAGEMENT

During a backup of the Information and Directory Stores, the Key Management server data is not backed up. To accomplish this, you need to stop the Key Management service and backup \EXCHSRVR\KMS-DATA manually.

If you have opted to use the Key Management server startup disk, you should back this disk up regularly as well. If you lose the disk or the disk fails, the service will not start.

To restore Key Management server services you must do the following:

1. Stop the Key Management service.
2. Restore the \EXCHSRVR\KMSDATA subdirectory.
3. Restore the startup disk.
4. Start the Key Management service.

WINDOWS NT REGISTRY

Under Microsoft Exchange 5.5, the services and connector information are stored in the Windows NT Registry. If your Exchange service account is deleted or a database is corrupt, you will need to restore it. You cannot

create the exact same Exchange service account due to the security identi-
fiers (SIDs) being different. If your Windows NT Registry is not backed
up, you'll have to reinstall every server that uses the specified Exchange
service account. For this reason, it's vital to maintain up to date backups
of the NT Registry.

To restore the Windows NT Registry follow these steps:

1. Start **NTBACKUP**.

2. Select the backup tape you want to restore from.

3. Click **Restore**.

4. Select the **Restore Local Registry** option.

TESTING YOUR BACKUP CHOICES

The best backup is only as good as the worst restore. There is no purpose
in backing up your Microsoft Exchange 5.5 server if you don't test the
restore process. You don't want to discover a step you weren't prepared
for when you're actually trying to restore information.

On a regular basis, preferably monthly, you should test your restore procedures on a test network with a test server that should replicate production
as much as possible. You should test three different restore scenarios:

1. **Full Restore of Microsoft Exchange 5.5 and Windows NT
   Server**—This option is for catastrophic failures of your entire
   server.

2. **Full Restore of Microsoft Exchange 5.5**—This option is for
   systemic or database corruption of your Microsoft Exchange 5.5
   installation.

3. **Full Restore of Windows NT Server**—This option is for
   Registry or system file issues. This is good to test just in case a
   Service Pack or patch goes awry.

Testing of your restore procedures is crucial for three reasons:

1. **Equipment on Hand**—Testing ensures you have the proper restore equipment on hand.

2. **Tape Validity**—Testing ensures that your tapes and tape formats are valid.

3. **Time to Restore**—Testing gives you a baseline for how long a restore will take. Nothing is more frustrating to your users than being told the server will be up in two hours, when in reality they have to wait all day.

In this lesson, you've learned about backup types, the NTBACKUP.EXE program, and restoring your Microsoft Exchange 5.5 installation.

LESSON 15

CLIENT TROUBLE-SHOOTING GUIDE

In this lesson, you'll learn how to properly troubleshoot, solve, and satisfy client issues.

Just as Microsoft Exchange 5.5 is a complex, evolutionary product, Outlook 98 is revolutionary. Outlook 98 brings a whole new level of complexity and dynamics to the simple email client. Sending and receiving email has been augmented with a full-blown Personal Information Manager. What was once very simple to support becomes much more difficult.

Let's face it, though. About 99 percent of your users aren't going to complain too much if they can't use the Notes section of Outlook 98. More likely, 99 percent of your users will complain if they can't send and receive email.

By using the techniques in this lesson you'll be able to solve most of your basic Outlook 98 issues.

WHEN GOOD PROFILES GO BAD

Outlook 98 uses *profiles* to manage its configuration. A profile is a collection of services. Services can be used to connect to various email servers such as Microsoft Exchange 5.5 Server, CompuServe email, and Internet email among others.

Outlook 98 creates a default profile called Microsoft Outlook when it is installed. Typically, you would add services to this profile. When

troubleshooting, I recommend you create a new profile with the Microsoft
Exchange 5.5 service only. This allows you to rule out interference with
another service.

 A Close Call   You should close Outlook 98before you
modify or create new profiles.

CREATING A NEW PROFILE

To create a new profile you will need to complete the following steps:

1. Select from the **Start** menu, select **Settings, Control Panel,** and
   you will see a window similar to the one in Figure 15.1.

FIGURE **15.1**   The Control Panel window.

2. Double-click the **Mail** icon and you will see the Properties
   screen (see Figure 15.2), which allows you to access the default
   Microsoft Outlook profile.

3. In the Microsoft Outlook Properties dialog box, select the **Show
   Profiles** button. You'll then see a dialog box displaying a list of
   one or more profiles, such as the one in Figure 15.3.

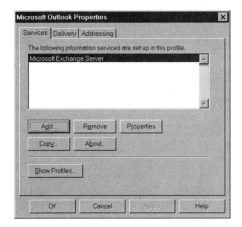

FIGURE 15.2   The Microsoft Outlook Profile Properties dialog box.

FIGURE 15.3   Displaying all available profiles.

4. Click **Add**, and a Setup Wizard will open. Click the **Use the Following Information Services** radio button (see Figure 15.4), and then click **Microsoft Exchange Server**. Click **Next**.

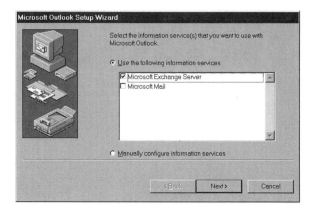

FIGURE 15.4   The Outlook Setup Wizard.

5. In the Profile Name text box, enter a name for the profile (see Figure 15.5). You should name it something such as *Test* or *Trouble*. Click **Next**.

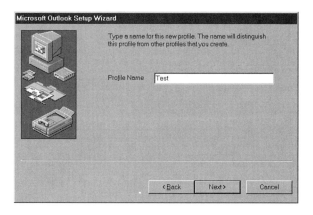

FIGURE 15.5   Setting the Microsoft Outlook profile name.

6. You will now be prompted to enter the Microsoft Exchange Server and mailbox names. Enter the information as shown in Figure 15.6. When you're finished, click **Next**.

FIGURE **15.6**   Entering the Microsoft Exchange Server name and mailbox.

7. At this point, the Setup Wizard inquires about using this computer for remote email. Enter information based on the current setup. For purposes of this example, click the **No** radio button, as in Figure 15.7. Click **Next**.

FIGURE **15.7**   Choosing local or remote mail.

8. After you do so, click **OK**. The Mail setup screen will then appear again. You need to select the new Profile you created under the field, When Starting Microsoft Outlook, Use This Profile, as shown in Figure 15.8.

> **Little Black Virtual Book**   At this point, depending
> on whether you already have a mail client installed,
> you might receive a dialog box asking you to enter a
> path to your Personal Address Book. If so, enter the
> path or click Browse to locate your existing client's
> address book.

FIGURE **15.8**   Selecting the alternative profile.

At this point, you have done the following:

- Verified and entered the correct server name and user mailbox

- Verified whether the mail is local or remote

- Created a new troubleshooting profile

- Selected the new profile to be used when Outlook 98 starts the
next time

Your next step is loading Outlook 98 and testing the new profile. If there
is a profile or service issue with the old profile, you will know if this profile and service works.

If creating a new profile and service fixed the Outlook 98 client problem, you can either leave things as they are or rename the new profile to the same name as the old profile. You might want to do this depending on your standards.

To rename a profile, though, you have to do a little work, because Microsoft didn't include a rename function for their profiles. To rename a profile, you'll actually delete the old profile, copy a profile, and then delete a profile again. Follow these steps:

1. Select the **Start** menu, click **Settings**, and launch the **Control Panel**; you will see the Control Panel screen, similar to the one in Figure 15.9.

FIGURE **15.9** The Control Panel.

2. Double-click the **Mail** icon and you will see the Properties dialog box, as shown in Figure 15.10, which shows the current Microsoft Outlook profile.

3. In the Microsoft Outlook Properties screen, select the **Show Profiles** button. You'll then see a list of profiles similar to the one in Figure 15.11.

4. Select the old profile—typically Microsoft Outlook—and then click **Remove**. You will then be prompted to verify your choice, as shown in Figure 15.12.

FIGURE 15.10   The Microsoft Outlook Profile Properties dialog box.

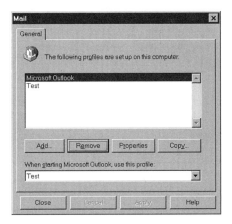

FIGURE 15.11   Displaying all available profiles.

FIGURE 15.12   Verify removal of the old profile.

5. Click **Yes** to remove the profile, and then highlight the profile you created to troubleshoot it. Select the **Copy** command and enter `Microsoft Outlook`, as shown in Figure 15.13. Click **OK** when you're finished.

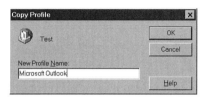

FIGURE 15.13   Copying and assigning a new name to a profile.

6. You'll now see there are two profiles. Select the **Microsoft Outlook** profile in the field When Starting Microsoft Outlook, Use this profile, as in Figure 15.14.

FIGURE 15.14   Using the new profile for Outlook 98.

Profiles and services are common sources of trouble for end users. The steps you just followed are a good start toward fixing these woes.

Networking issues are another source of trouble that should be examined. They are discussed in the following sections.

ANYONE OUT THERE?

Sometimes your Outlook 98 configuration will be perfect, but you still can't access the Microsoft Exchange 5.5 Server. At that point, you should verify that you have network connectivity with the Microsoft Exchange 5.5 Server.

Most installations use TCP/IP as their network protocol. For this reason, I'll be using TCP/IP as the example for troubleshooting network communication issues.

Your first goal is to ensure the client computer has a TCP/IP address assigned to it. Depending on whether you are troubleshooting a Windows NT 4.0 or Windows 95/98 client, there are two different utility programs you can use. I'll discuss each one in turn.

VERIFYING TCP/IP INFORMATION ON A WINDOWS NT 4.0 CLIENT

To verify your TCP/IP Information, follow these steps:

1. Select the **Start** menu, choose **Programs**, and then click **Command Prompt**, as shown in Figure 15.15, to enter the command-based console of Windows NT.

2. You can access the TCP/IP information by typing **IPCONFIG** at the command prompt. You will be shown the TCP/IP information in a screen similar to the one in Figure 15.6.

You should see your TCP/IP address, subnet mask and default gateway. If you don't see this information, you might have to install the TCP/IP protocol. I'll cover that later in this lesson.

Before you reinstall the TCP/IP protocol, check the cable connection to the client. Ensure the cable is secure in the socket of the NIC with a link light, if one is available.

FIGURE 15.15   Opening the Windows NT 4.0 Command Prompt.

```
Command Prompt                                              _ □ X
Microsoft(R) Windows NT(TM)
(C) Copyright 1985-1996 Microsoft Corp.

C:\>ipconfig

Windows NT IP Configuration

Ethernet adapter AMDPCN1:

        IP Address. . . . . . . . . : 192.168.0.33
        Subnet Mask . . . . . . . . : 255.255.255.0
        Default Gateway . . . . . . : 192.168.0.1

C:\>
```

FIGURE 15.16   Using IPCONFIG to verify Windows NT 4.0 settings.

VERIFYING TCP/IP INFORMATION ON A WINDOWS 95/98 CLIENT

To verify your TCP/IP information, follow these steps:

1. Select the Start menu and choose Run.

2. Enter the program **WINIPCFG**. Hit Enter and you will receive a screen like the one in Figure 15.17.

FIGURE 15.17   WINIPCFG under Windows 95/98.

You should see your TCP/IP address, subnet mask and default gateway. If you don't see this information, you will have to install the TCP/IP protocol. I'll cover that process later in this lesson.

Before you reinstall the TCP/IP protocol, check the cable connection to the client. Ensure the cable is secure in the socket of the NIC with a link light, if one is available.

TESTING TCP/IP CONNECTIVITY

After you've verified a TCP/IP address has been assigned to the client, you need to test the connection.

Testing the connectivity is best accomplished by using the PING command. The PING command sends packets of data from one TCP/IP client to another to verify connectivity. Think of it as if you are on the third story of a house and yelling down the stairs to see if someone is down on the first story.

You'll need to open a command prompt session on either Windows 95/98 or Windows NT 4.0. The PING commands work the same on each operating system.

By Your Command   You open a command prompt session by choosing the **Start** menu, selecting Programs, and selecting the MS-DOS Prompt command in Windows 95 and 98, or **Command Prompt** in Windows NT.

After the command prompt is active, follow these steps:

1. From the client's machine type **PING** *Client TCP/IP Address* (substitute the actual address for *client TCP/IP address*), and you should receive a result similar to the one in Figure 15.18. If you do, your internal TCP/IP functions are working. If you do not receive a successful ping, reinstall TCP/IP. (Again, I'll describe how to do so later.)

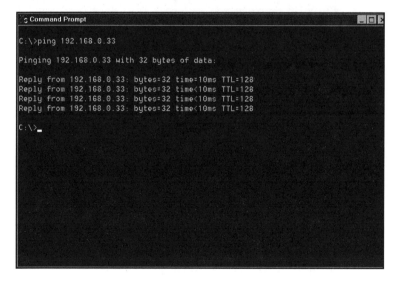

FIGURE **15.18**   Using PING to verify the client TCP/IP address.

2. From the client's machine, type **ping www.yahoo.com** and you should receive a result similar to Figure 15.19. If you do, your DNS and Internet connectivity is working. If you do not receive

a successful ping, reinstall TCP/IP. (Note: This example will
only work if your company offers direct access to the Internet. If
your company doesn't support direct access to the Internet, you
should attempt to ping a local Web or FTP server located on
your company network.)

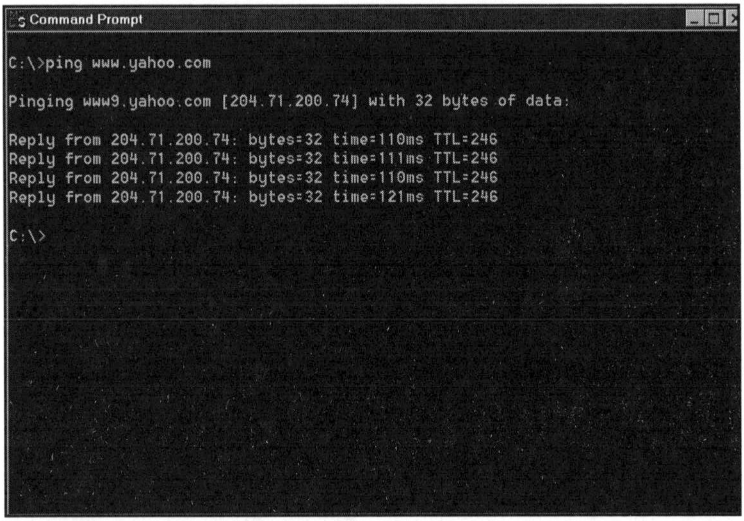

```
C:\>ping www.yahoo.com

Pinging www9.yahoo.com [204.71.200.74] with 32 bytes of data:

Reply from 204.71.200.74: bytes=32 time=110ms TTL=246
Reply from 204.71.200.74: bytes=32 time=111ms TTL=246
Reply from 204.71.200.74: bytes=32 time=110ms TTL=246
Reply from 204.71.200.74: bytes=32 time=121ms TTL=246

C:\>
```

Figure 15.19   Using PING to verify the client can resolve DNS
requests and access the network.

Adding TCP/IP to the Client Computer

TCP/IP is necessary for communicating and transferring email with
Microsoft Exchange 5.5. If your TCP/IP installation is invalid or if
TCP/IP isn't installed (which you will have determined in the preceding
exercises), you will need to install it.

Make sure you test the TCP/IP installation after installation by using the
PING command.

ADDING TCP/IP TO WINDOWS NT 4.0

Normally, TCP/IP is the default protocol for Windows NT 4.0. In case it is missing or if you feel the installation might be corrupt, you can reinstall it. The process of adding TCP/IP to Windows NT 4.0 is straightforward. Follow these commands to complete the installation:

1. Select the **Start** menu, choose **Settings**, and launch the **Control Panel**; you will see the Control Panel applet icons.

2. Double-click the **Network** icon, and you will see the Properties dialog box shown in Figure 15.20.

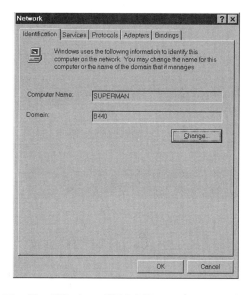

FIGURE 15.20   The Windows NT 4.0 Network properties window.

3. Click on the **Protocols** tab, and then select the **Add** option. You will see the dialog box in Figure 15.21.

4. Choose the **TCP/IP Protocol** and select **OK**. A dialog box asking if you use a DHCP server on your network appears, as shown in Figure 15.22. DHCP is an automated method for assigning TCP/IP addresses to clients. This prevents TCP/IP

addresses from having to be hard-coded to each workstation. If
you have DHCP, click **OK**, and you will be prompted to restart
the computer.

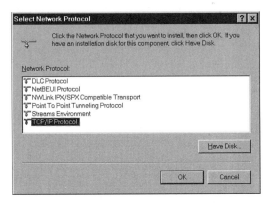

FIGURE 15.21   Adding a protocol to Windows NT 4.0.

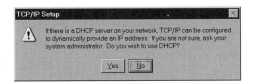

FIGURE 15.22   Do you use DHCP?

5. If you select **No**, Windows NT 4.0 will need to copy system files
   from the original Windows NT 4.0 CD-ROM. Enter the location
   of your I386 subdirectory at the prompt, as in Figure 15.23, and
   press **Enter**.

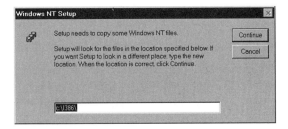

FIGURE 15.23   Specifying the location of your I386 subdirectory.

CDs of Trouble Sometimes people misplace their original system CD-ROMs. Can you imagine that? If you can, you might want to copy the I386 subdirectory from your CD-ROM to your server's C: drive so it is always available.

6. After Windows NT 4.0 copies over the files needed for TCP/IP, you will be prompted for the client computer's TCP/IP configuration. You will need to enter your IP address information in the Microsoft TCP/IP Properties dialog box, as shown in Figure 15.24. You will need to enter the IP address, subnet mask and default gateway.

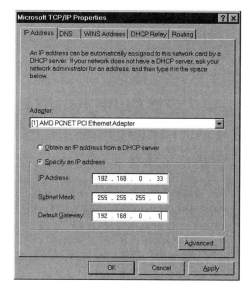

FIGURE 15.24   Entering your client TCP/IP address information.

7. If your site uses DNS, select the **DNS** tab before you click **OK** or **Apply**. You will need to enter your hostname, domain, and DNS search order, as shown in Figure 15.25.

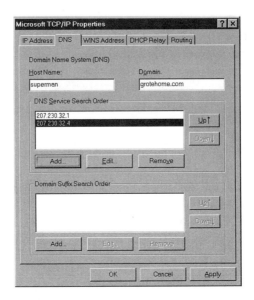

FIGURE 15.25   Entering your client DNS information.

8. After you've entered the DNS information, click **OK**. Windows
   NT 4.0 will reprocess the binding information and you will be
   prompted to restart your computer, as shown in Figure 15.26.

FIGURE 15.26   Complete the installation of TCP/IP by restarting your
computer.

You have finished installing TCP/IP for Windows NT 4.0. You should now
attempt to test the TCP/IP installation by using the PING command as
described earlier.

ADDING TCP/IP TO WINDOWS 95/98

Adding TCP/IP to Windows 95/98 is a simple process. Follow these commands:

1. Open the Control Panel by clicking on the **Start** menu, choosing **Settings**, and clicking **Control Panel**.

2. Double-click the **Network** icon to open the applet. You'll see a screen similar to the one Figure 15.27 that details the installed network services.

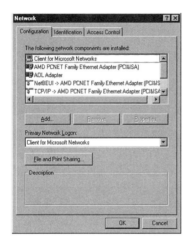

FIGURE **15.27**   The Network applet in Windows 95/98.

3. Select **Add**, and you will be prompted to make a selection by the Select Network Component Type dialog box. Highlight the protocol choice as in Figure 15.28.

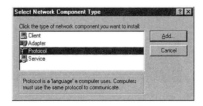

FIGURE **15.28**   Selecting the network component to install.

4. Clicking **Add** displays a list of vendors and protocols. Select **Microsoft** from the list on the left and highlight **TCP/IP** on the right side of the screen, as shown in Figure 15.29.

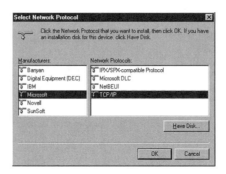

FIGURE 15.29   Selecting Microsoft's TCP/IP to install in Windows 95/98.

5. After the installation routine copies files, you are presented with the TCP/IP Properties screen, shown in Figure 15.30. You need to enter the IP address and subnet mask for this client (don't use the information in the example).

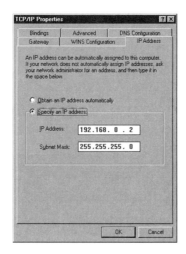

FIGURE 15.30   Entering the IP address information in Windows 95/98.

6. Before clicking **OK**, you'll need to enter two more configuration items. The first is the Gateway. Select the **Gateway** tab on top of the TCP/IP Properties window. You'll be presented with the Gateway options, as shown in Figure 15.31. Enter the gateway information as appropriate for the workstation in question.

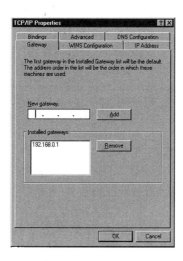

FIGURE **15.31** Entering the gateway information in Windows 95/98.

7. If your site uses DNS, select the **DNS Configuration** tab on top of the TCP/IP Properties window. You'll be presented with the DNS Configuration options, as shown in Figure 15.32. Enter the DNS information.

After you have completed entering the information, click **OK**. Windows 95/98 will complete copying the files and will prompt you to restart the computer. Select **OK** at this prompt and wait for the computer to restart.

At this point, you have finished installing TCP/IP for Windows NT 95/98. You should test the TCP/IP installation by using the PING command as I described earlier.

In this lesson you learned how to troubleshoot and fix common client issues with profiles, services, TCP/IP, and the network.

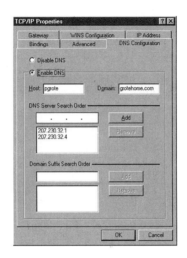

FIGURE 15.32   Entering the DNS configuration information in
Windows 95/98.

LESSON 16

MICROSOFT EXCHANGE 5.5 SERVER TROUBLESHOOTING

In this lesson, you will learn to troubleshoot common issues on the server side that arise from the daily use of Microsoft Exchange 5.5.

Troubleshooting Microsoft Exchange 5.5 Server issues is sometimes a hard task. With Windows NT Server 4.0 providing the underlying network operating system, it is important to try to differentiate between Microsoft Exchange 5.5 Server issues and Windows NT Server 4.0 issues.

Usually your Exchange users will bring most of the issues that occur to your attention. Issues that affect the sending and receiving of email receive the highest attention by users.

There are two tools that can help you troubleshoot these message delivery issues:

1. Message tracking
2. Diagnostic logging

MESSAGE TRACKING

Message tracking allows you to follow a message through the Microsoft Exchange 5.5 internal infrastructure. By doing this, you can troubleshoot the following issues:

- **Lost Mail**—Users might complain that messages they are sending to another recipient are not being delivered, and yet they don't receive a non-delivery message from Microsoft Exchange 5.5.

- **Slow Delivery**—Users might complain that messages that should be delivered instantaneously are taking 10 or more minutes (or a similar lengthy period) to be delivered.

- **Non-Delivery**—Users might complain that messages are being returned to them with a non-delivery error.

ENABLING MESSAGE TRACKING

The first step in using message tracking is to enable it. When you install Microsoft Exchange 5.5, this feature is not enabled.

The components under which message tracking can be enabled are as follows:

- Message Transfer Agent

- Information Store

- Internet Mail Service

- cc:Mail Connector

- MS Mail Connector

For example purposes, enable message tracking on the Message Transfer Agent, Information Store, and Internet Mail Service.

 Maxing Out Your CPU   Message tracking is a powerful feature of Microsoft Exchange 5.5, but it is extremely CPU-intensive. You should only enable and use it when you need to troubleshoot a specific issue.

ENABLING MESSAGE TRACKING FOR THE INFORMATION STORE

The Information Store contains the user messages for the Microsoft Exchange 5.5 Server. Complete the following steps to enable message tracking on this component:

1. Open the Exchange Administrator program by selecting the **Start** menu, clicking **Programs, Microsoft Exchange, Microsoft Exchange Administrator,** as shown in Figure 16.1.

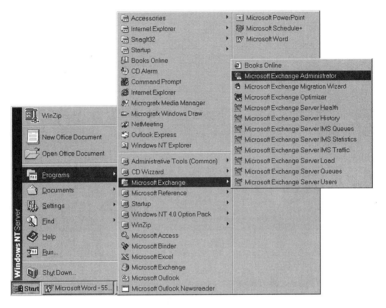

FIGURE 16.1   Starting the Microsoft Exchange Administrator.

2. Select the site where message tracking will be enabled. Select the **Configuration** container by double-clicking it. You will see the configuration objects appear on the right of the window, as shown in Figure 16.2

3. Double-click the **Information Store Site Configuration** object and, in the resulting dialog box, enable the **Enable Message Tracking** option under the General tab, as shown in Figure 16.3. Click **OK.**

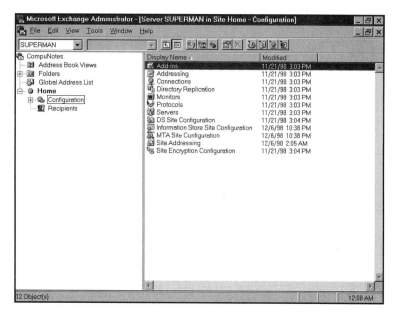

FIGURE 16.2   Selecting the proper site and configuration container.

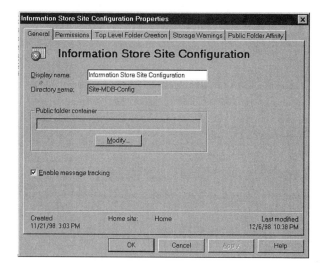

FIGURE 16.3   Enabling the message tracking function under the
Information Store.

ENABLING MESSAGE TRACKING FOR THE MESSAGE TRACKING AGENT

The Message Tracking Agent (MTA) performs the email routing for the Microsoft Exchange 5.5 Server. You enable message tracking for the MTA by following a similar procedure to the one you just used for the Information Store:

1. Open the Exchange Administrator program by selecting the **Start** menu, and clicking **Programs, Microsoft Exchange, Microsoft Exchange Administrator** (refer to Figure 16.1).

2. Select the site where message tracking will be enabled. Double-click the **Configuration** container. You will see the configuration objects appear on the right of the window (refer to Figure 16.2).

3. Double-click the **MTA Site Configuration** object and enable the **Enable Message Tracking** option under the General tab as in Figure 16.4. Click **OK**.

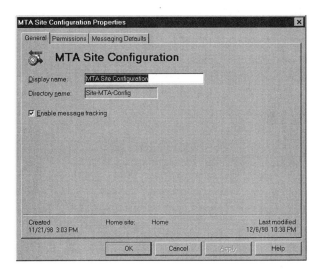

FIGURE 16.4   Enabling message tracking under the Mail Transfer Agent.

ENABLING MESSAGE TRACKING FOR THE INTERNET MAIL SERVICE

For message tracking to work successfully, it must be enabled on each of your Internet Mail Service servers. Typically, your organization will have only one Internet Mail Service server, but if you have more than one, you'll need to enable it on each by following these steps:

1. Open the Exchange Administrator program by selecting the **Start** menu, clicking **Programs**, choosing the **Microsoft Exchange** group, and launching **Microsoft Exchange Administrator**.

2. Select the site with the Internet Mail Service and double-click it. Double-click the **Configuration** container, and then double-click the **Connections** container. You will see a window similar to the one in Figure 16.5, with the Connections object on the right side.

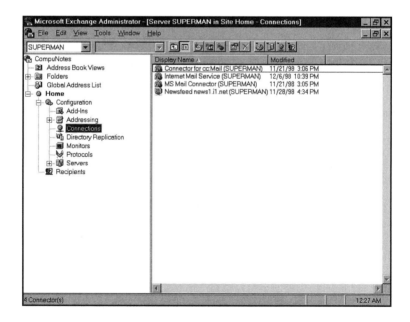

FIGURE 16.5   The Connections objects under Microsoft Exchange Administrator.

3. Double-click the **Internet Mail Service** object, and then enable the **Enable Message Tracking** option under the Internet Mail Tab, as shown in Figure 16.6.

FIGURE 16.6   Enabling message tracking under Internet Mail Service using Microsoft Exchange Administrator.

After message tracking is enabled, you'll need to restart the Microsoft Exchange 5.5 Server so the services can be reloaded.

Off Track   Because message tracking uses logs to track messages, you won't be able to track messages that have been sent prior to enabling message tracking. These previous messages would not have left a log trail.

SELECTING A MESSAGE TO TRACK

Congratulations on enabling message tracking! You'll now use the Track Messages command in Exchange Administrator to search the daily tracking logs for specific message status.

Follow these steps to track a message:

1. Open the Exchange Administrator program by selecting the **Start** menu, and selecting **Programs, Microsoft Exchange, Microsoft Exchange Administrator**.

2. Select the **Track Messages** command from the **Tool** menu, as in Figure 16.7.

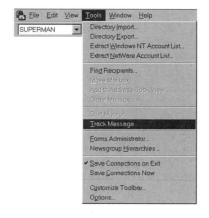

FIGURE **16.7** Selecting the Track Message command using Exchange Administrator.

3. If you haven't selected a default Exchange server to administer, you will be prompted for the Exchange server, as shown in Figure 16.8. Enter the name of the server or use the browse function, and click **OK** to continue.

FIGURE 16.8   Selecting the Exchange Server to administer.

4. The Select Message to Track dialog box now appears. This dialog box is used to set the criteria that will be used to search for messages. You can base your search on the author of the message or the recipient. You can also specify how many days back you want to search. Enter a mailbox name in the To or From field and leave the Look Back field at 0, as in Figure 16.9.

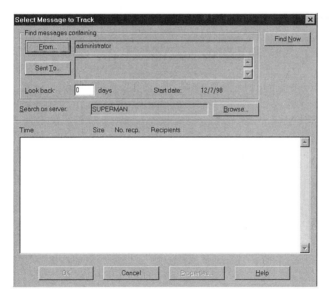

FIGURE 16.9   Setting the criteria for a message search.

5. Click the Find Now button and your search is executed. As the search works through the log files, you will see a status display similar to the one in Figure 16.10.

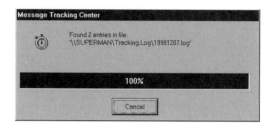

FIGURE 16.10   A message search is being executed.

6. After the search has completed, you will see a screen similar to the one in Figure 16.11. Notice the results of the search now appear on the bottom part of the screen. The listed messages are available to be tracked.

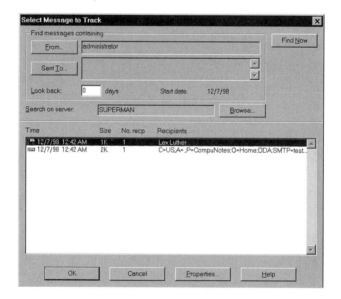

FIGURE 16.11   A message search is completed with the results displayed.

7. You can now view information about each message by either
   double-clicking it or selecting it and clicking **Properties**. After
   you have selected the message, you will see detailed information
   similar to that shown in Figure 16.12.

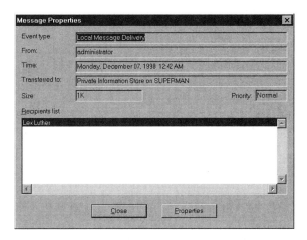

FIGURE 16.12   Detailed properties of a message found in the
search.

THE MESSAGE TRACKING CENTER

After you have found a message using the Message to Track dialog box,
you can trace its path through the Microsoft Exchange 5.5 infrastructure
using the Message Tracking Center. The Message Tracking Center traces
the path of the message through the logs of all the servers that handle the
message. The Message Tracking Center completes its search when the
message leaves the local network or is successfully delivered.

To use the Message Tracking Center, highlight one of the found messages
in the Select Messages to Track dialog box, and then click **OK**.

After you return to the Message Tracking Center, click the **Tracking** button. The Message Tracking Center will then search all the applicable logs
and detail its results in the Tracking History windows (see Figure 16.13).

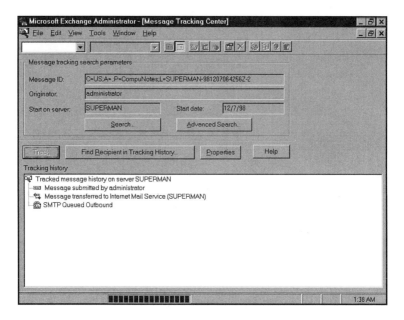

FIGURE 16.13   Tracking a message using the Message Tracking Center.

Notice the trail of status messages under the Tracking History window. You can receive more detailed information on any of the status reports by highlighting it and clicking the **Properties** button. You'll see a status screen similar to the one in Figure 16.14.

Each of the status reports in the Message Tracking Center corresponds to a processing event in your Microsoft Exchange 5.5 infrastructure.

Advanced Search is another method for searching for messages. By clicking on the **Advanced Search** button on the Message Tracking Center, you can search for messages based on the following criteria, as shown in Figure 16.15:

- **Sent by Microsoft Exchange Server**—If one of the components of Microsoft Exchange 5.5 sends a status message, you can track its delivery using this option.

- **Transferred Into this Site**—This option allows you to track the messages that did not originate at the current site. This is a good option for tracking site-to-site issues.

- **By Message ID**—Each Microsoft Exchange 5.5 message is
  assigned an ID. If you know the ID of the message you would
  like to track, you can enter it here.

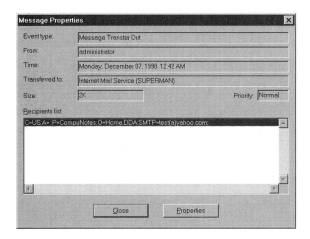

FIGURE 16.14   Details on a status report in the Message Tracking
Center.

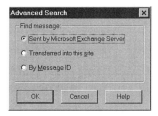

FIGURE 16.15   Setting advanced message tracking criteria.

Message tracking is a powerful option for finding out what happened to
messages after Microsoft Exchange 5.5 receives them.

DIAGNOSTIC LOGGING

Imagine being able to receive in-depth information about the inner work-
ings of your Microsoft Exchange 5.5 Server. Imagine being able to

pinpoint when a subsystem breaks down in the Microsoft Exchange 5.5 Server. Imagine no more. You have this functionality with *diagnostic logging.*

Diagnostic logging allows you to receive status reports from certain functions in Microsoft Exchange 5.5. Using these status reports, you can piece together a process flow or troubleshoot issues.

DIAGNOSTIC LEVELS

There are various levels of diagnostic logging. Each level is assigned a value from 0–5, where 0 is a system critical error. The difference in levels equates to how much information is being sent in each status report. There are four levels of diagnostic logging:

1. **None**—The event level is 0. Under this default setting, only critical events are logged. You should use this level on a daily basis if the system is functioning properly.

2. **Minimum**—The event level is 1. Upper-level events are logged. You should use this level to begin troubleshooting your issues.

3. **Medium**—The event level is 4. Task level events are logged. You should use this level when you have a strong idea of what is wrong.

4. **Maximum**—The event level is 5. All events related to a task are logged. This level's price has a severe performance effect on Microsoft Exchange 5.5. You should use this setting to view one object a time.

 Watch Your Disk Space   Event levels 4 and 5 consume a large amount of disk space. Be prepared to clean your event log out daily to ensure your Windows NT 4.0 Server continues proper operation.

COMPONENT DIAGNOSTICS

Microsoft Exchange 5.5 doesn't support diagnostic logging on all components. It doesn't make sense to log events through components that don't affect your messages. The following components do support diagnostic logging:

- **Private Information Store**—You can enable Diagnostic Logging by highlighting Private Information Store under the Server container and viewing properties. You will see a Properties screen such as the one in Figure 16.16 when you select the **Diagnostics** tab.

FIGURE 16.16   Setting the level of diagnostic logging for the Private Information Store.

- **Public Information Store**—You can enable diagnostic logging by highlighting **Public Information Store** under the **Server** container and viewing **Properties**. You will see a dialog box similar to the one in Figure 16.17 when you select the **Diagnostics Logging** tab.

FIGURE 16.17   Setting the level of diagnostic logging for the Public Information Store.

- **Directory Service**—You can enable diagnostic logging by high-lighting **Directory Service** under the **Server** container and viewing **Properties**. You will see a Properties screen similar to the one in Figure 16.18 when you select the **Diagnostics Logging** tab.

- **Directory Synchronization**—You can enable Diagnostic Logging by highlighting **Directory Synchronization** under the **Server** container and viewing **Properties**. You will see a dialog box such as the one in Figure 16.19 when you select the **Diagnostics Logging** tab.

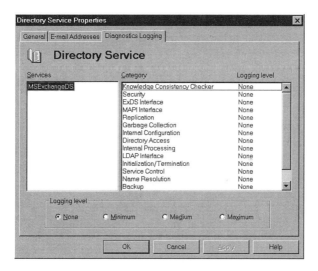

FIGURE 16.18   Setting the level of diagnostic logging for Directory Service.

FIGURE 16.19   Setting the level of diagnostic logging for Directory Synchronization.

- **Message Transfer Agent**—You can enable diagnostic logging by highlighting **Message Transfer Agent** under the **Server** container and viewing **Properties**. You will see a Properties screen such as the one in Figure 16.20 when you select the **Diagnostics Logging** tab.

FIGURE **16.20**   Setting the level of diagnostic logging for the Message Transfer Agent.

- **Internet Mail Service**—You can enable diagnostic logging by highlighting **Internet Mail Service** under the **Connections** container and viewing **Properties**. You will see a Properties dialog box similar to the one in Figure 16.21 when you select the **Diagnostics Logging** tab.

There are two other components that support diagnostic logging:

- cc:Mail connector
- MS Mail connector

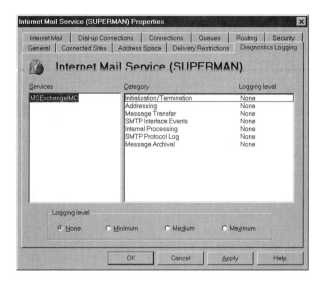

FIGURE **16.21**   Setting the level of diagnostic logging for the Internet Mail Service.

VIEWING THE RESULTS

Now that you've enabled diagnostic logging on your components, you'll need to see the results. Using the Windows NT Server 4.0 Event Viewer, you can see the results of the diagnostic logging.

You can run the Event Viewer by following these steps:

1. Select the **Start** menu.

2. Click **Programs**.

3. Choose the **Administrative Tools (common)** group.

4. Click **Event Viewer** to launch the program, as shown in Figure 16.22.

Figure 16.23 shows an example Event Viewer with a log of errors.

Diagnostic logging is a very useful tool if managed properly. Ensure that you are pruning your logs regularly, so that disk space doesn't become limited.

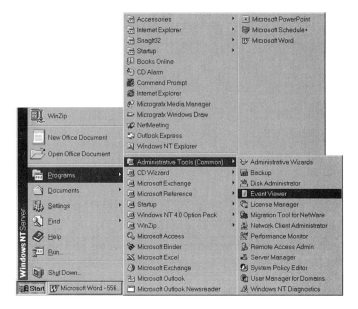

FIGURE 16.22   Loading the Windows NT Server 4.0 Event Viewer.

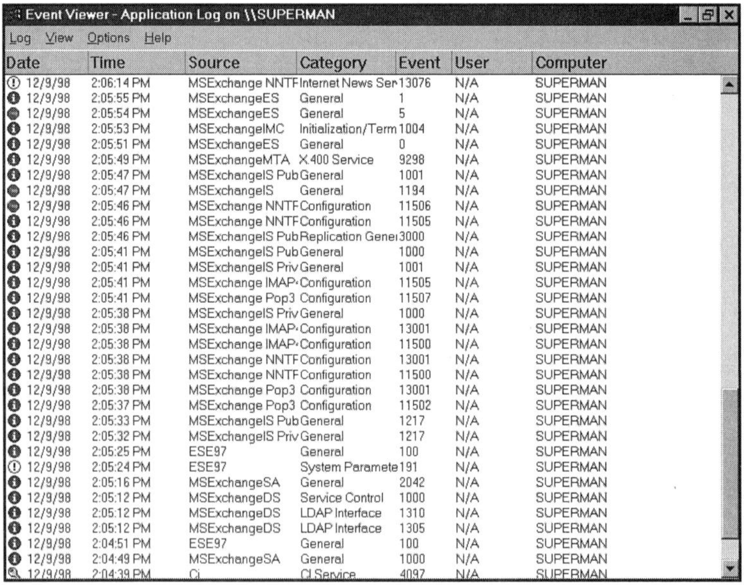

FIGURE 16.23   Viewing the diagnostic log using the Event Viewer.

In this lesson, you learned how to troubleshoot server-related Microsoft Exchange 5.5 issues using message tracking and diagnostic logging.

LESSON 17
KEY
MANAGEMENT
SERVER

In this lesson you'll learn about the public/private key encryption technology called Key Management Server and how it works with Microsoft Exchange 5.5.

After Microsoft Exchange 5.5 is up and running in your organization, you will notice that it is very good at sending and receiving email. One of the more underrated features of Microsoft Exchange 5.5 is the Key Management Server (KMS).

One of the problems with email communications is that, without extra software, it is not secure. Sure, you can use *encryption* to keep your email private, but you can never be sure that the person who sent an email message is who they claim to be. This is especially true with email sent across the Internet.

Encryption The process of turning a plain text message into a coded or cipher message. Encryption is used to secure the text so only those users with a decryption tool can decode the message and convert it back into plain text.

Authentication The process used to verify that a user is who they claim to be. Simple authentication methods rely on a username and password, whereas advanced authentication methods rely on a thumbprint or voice password.

KMS brings two new security features to Microsoft Exchange 5.5 that you should be aware of:

1. **Signing**—This allows a sender to digitally sign the message with an electronic signature. The signature is unique and registered to the sender. Think of it as a digital fingerprint.

2. **Sealing**—This allows a sender to encrypt the message and attachments, which effectively makes the message unreadable to people who cannot decrypt it. Think of it as scrambling your message into code.

These features are based on industry standard encryption methods called public/private key technology.

Public/private key technology is exactly what it sounds like. Two mathematically related keys, public and private, are supplied to lock and unlock messages. Without these keys, reading the message is impossible. Even if you randomly tried different keys it would take over one trillion keys to find the proper one.

 Further Reading   Cryptography is a fascinating subject, especially as it applies to computers. Standards are still evolving under the watchful eye of governments. For more information, try searching for the keyword cryptography on the Internet, or try your local library or bookstore.

Public Keys

KMS uses public keys as a security device for all users to accomplish the following:

- **Seal Messages**—The first public key is used to scramble or encrypt the message. When the message is encrypted, it is termed as sealed.

- **Verify Messages**—The second public key is used to verify the sender of the mail message. This is important to ensure the validity of the identity of the sender.

PRIVATE KEYS

KMS uses private keys as a security device for individual users to accomplish the following:

- **Sign Messages**—The first private key is used by the sender to digitally sign the message. This secures the message and provides the proof necessary to ensure the message is actually from the sender.

- **Decrypt Messages**—The second private key is used to decrypt received messages.

To understand how this process works, envision the following example:

Patrick has a confidential status report he needs to send to Roger over the Internet. To ensure the message is encrypted, Patrick uses Roger's public key to secure the message, and if Patrick decides to sign the message, he uses his own private key. The message is now encrypted and signed.

After the message is delivered to Roger, he uses Patrick's public key to verify that Patrick did indeed send the message. Roger then uses his private key to decrypt and read the message in plain text.

There is a very important point to note about how Microsoft Exchange 5.5 and KMS handle the decryption process. When the client decrypts a message, it is not decrypted and stored in the users Inbox. It is temporarily decrypted in memory, which adds to the more secure nature of encrypted messages.

THE LOCKSMITH

With all these public and private keys floating around, you'll need a way of organizing, storing, and accessing them. Microsoft Exchange 5.5 provides an integrated featured that handles the administration of keys for you. KMS is used to manage the advanced security features of Microsoft Exchange 5.5.

KMS is a bit of a misnomer, as it includes both server- and client-based components.

KEY MANAGEMENT SERVER COMPONENTS

KMS installs and uses three distinct components on the Microsoft Exchange 5.5 Server:

1. **Service**—The Key Management Service is run on startup and provides certificate authority. This means it creates and manages the Key Management database of keys. Certain actions, such as revoking or recovering a user's key, are available through the service.

2. **DLL**—The file SECKM.DLL is located on the server and is used for communication between the client and server for key-based requests.

3. **Database**—KMS needs a large database to store the necessary keys.

You should also know the following about the Key Management Server:

- You can only have one Key Management Server in your Microsoft Exchange 5.5 organization. This is due to the highly secure nature of key management.

- Key Management Server is language-based. You'll have to enter your country code when installing KMS. Typically, this will be the United State, but you might need another country. Because the United States and other countries might restrict the type of encryption that can be used, you should verify the legality of using KMS.

- To ensure a highly secure environment, you can designate a KMS administrator who is different than the Microsoft Exchange 5.5 administrator.

KEY MANAGEMENT SERVER CLIENT COMPONENTS

The Key Management Server installs and uses two distinct components on the Microsoft Exchange 5.5 client:

1. **Client Key DLL**—This DLL file provides the capability to sign, verify, seal, and unseal messages on the client. ETEXCH.DLL is used for 16-bit operating systems, and ETEXCH32.DLL is used for 32-bit operating systems.

2. **Security Administration DLL**—This DLL is used on the Exchange administrator's workstation to provide advanced security configuration.

Key Management Server is one of the more complex features of Microsoft Exchange 5.5. You'll need to adequately plan your security settings and review your internal security documents.

After you've implemented Key Management Server, your entire Microsoft Exchange 5.5 installation needs to be very secure. Because KMS provides data encryption, it is very well protected from intrusion with passwords and unorthodox control methods.

You need to ensure the rest of your Microsoft Exchange 5.5 installation is as secure as it can be. There are a few things you can do to improve your security situation:

- **Changes Passwords Often**—Change your administrator and Exchange Service Account passwords often. This limits the ability of someone to hack into your account.

- **Complex Passwords**—Some administrators don't have the resources available to change passwords on all their servers in a timely manner. In this case, ensure you use very complex passwords that are a combination of case and character types.

- **Ensure your Console is Secure**—Windows NT Server 4.0 features the capability to run applications locally. This also opens up the server to attack. Ensure that you are using a screen saver with a password. Even something as simple as a blank screen.

- **Disable Old Users**—System maintenance is important. Part of your maintenance should be disabling old users so they cannot access the Microsoft Exchange 5.5 installation.

In this lesson you learned about public/private key technology, encryption/decryption, Key Management Server, and how to improve your server's security.

LESSON 18

MICROSOFT
EXCHANGE 5.5
FORMS

In this lesson you'll learn about the types of forms Microsoft Exchange 5.5 supports and the program you'll use to create them.

Electronic forms are an efficient method of replacing paperwork in your office with electronic equivalents. The benefits of electronic forms include:

- **Paperwork Elimination**—Paperwork is costly to process and store. By using electronic forms, all the data can be accessed via computer and stored inexpensively. Furthermore, backup copies and duplicates are also easier to create, route, and store.

- **Auditable Routing**—When paperwork is sent to multiple people for review, there is a good chance it will be delayed or lost. Without effort, there is no method of checking the status. By using electronic forms and routing, you can easily check the status of distribution.

- **Data Collection**—If you collect information through responses to a memo or survey, you have to enter the data into the database by hand. Using electronic forms, the data can be automatically entered into a database.

- **Interactivity**—Electronic forms can be interactive. An expense report that totals itself then routes to the appropriate manager and a request form that generates email to-do lists are examples of interactive forms.

FORM ARSENAL

Microsoft Exchange 5.5 supports the following types of forms:

- **Survey Forms**—Survey forms are used to collect data from the end user. Examples of survey forms include company feedback forms and employee review forms.

- **Report Forms**—Report forms are used for automating standard information query and distribution. Examples of report forms are inventory or message forms. Another example is the While You Were Out form used for reporting telephone messages (see Figure 18.1).

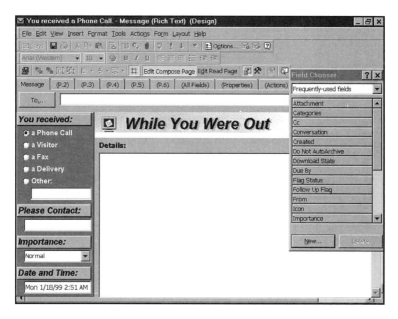

FIGURE **18.1**   This Exchange form can handle the duties of the humble paper message slip.

- **Request Form**—Request forms are used to automate requests typically submitted on paper. Examples of request forms include purchase orders and real estate move forms.

Your form can also specify the method in which it should be used. The Exchange library supports various methods including the following:

- **Organization Forms**—Server-based forms available to everyone in the organization

- **Personal Forms**—User-specific forms stored in the user's Inbox

- **Folder Forms**—Forms stored in public folders

CREATING FORMS

Creating forms for Microsoft Exchange 5.5 is client-based through Outlook 98. To access the Outlook 98 Forms Designer, use the following commands:

1. Open Outlook 98 and select the **Forms** pop-up menu from the **Tools** menu. At this point your screen will resemble the one shown in Figure 18.2.

FIGURE **18.2**   Starting the Forms Design process.

2. Select **Design a Form**, and the Forms Designer window, shown in Figure 18.3, appears.

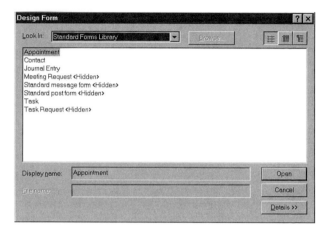

FIGURE 18.3   The Forms Designer.

The Forms Designer is your command center for designing and implementing forms for Microsoft Exchange 5.5. If you've ever designed forms in Microsoft Access, you'll recognize the process instantly; the two are very similar.

You have a wide selection of forms you can choose as a template, as shown in Figure 18.4.

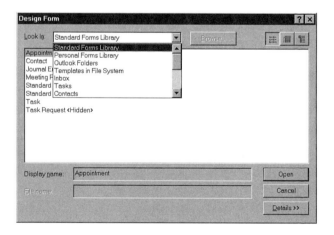

FIGURE 18.4   The Form Designer templates.

Outlook's Form Designer is a 32-bit program designed to bring collaboration and functionality to your Microsoft Exchange 5.5 installation. Essentially, you choose the type of fields you want to place on a form, and then drag, drop, and resize the fields on your blank form, as shown in Figure 18.5. You can create literally millions of combinations, enough for any business application.

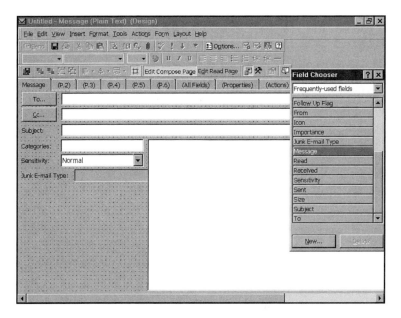

FIGURE **18.5** If the forms that come with Exchange don't quite fit your needs, you can custom-design your own.

In this lesson you learned about the forms Microsoft Exchange 5.5 supports and about the Forms Designer included with Outlook 98.

LESSON 19

DISASTER PREVENTION

In this lesson, you'll learn how to prevent disasters in your Microsoft Exchange 5.5 Server.

There are four areas you should focus on when preventing disasters in your Microsoft Exchange 5.5 installation:

- Environmental
- Hardware
- Software
- Maintenance

ENVIRONMENTAL DISASTER PREVENTION

For as much as computer equipment has improved, it is still an electronic device and should be treated as such. Make sure your server is not placed in an unstable environment. The best place for the server is on stable, well-built furniture or on a raised floor.

Sufficient power should be available. This doesn't mean ensuring there is just an outlet. You should also make sure that the power is clean and clear of spikes. An interruptible power source might not be a bad investment, depending on your budget.

Security is important as well. Ensure your server is behind a located door or is secure in another fashion. Keep controlled access logs to the room.

The temperature is another environmental condition to keep in mind. Servers generate a large amount of heat, so cool air must be constantly circulated in the room. A server that overheats can lead to processing or storage errors.

HARDWARE DISASTER PREVENTION

You can use hardware to help prevent disaster in your Microsoft Exchange 5.5 installation. The following hardware can help prevent disasters:

* Redundant power supplies

* UPS (uninteruptable power source)

* RAID (redundant array of inexpensive drives)

REDUNDANT POWER SUPPLIES

Losing all power completely because of a bad power supply is probably the worst thing that can happen to a server. Not many of us have extra power supplies lying around to use as a spare. With a server, the power supply is the most critical component to duplicate.

When you purchase a server, you should always ensure that it has redundant power supplies that automatically fail over in case power is interrupted.

UPS

A UPS ensures a steady stream of clean power is available to your server. A UPS will also prevent your server from being shut down if there is a power surge, spike, or temporary loss of power due to a storm or high winds.

Ensure you adequately plan for the drain on the UPS. You want a UPS that will supply power for the amount of time it takes to shut down your computer plus a comfortable safety margin. For example, if it takes 10 minutes for your Microsoft Exchange 5.5 Server to shut down properly, make sure you purchase a UPS that can provide 15 minutes of UPS time.

The Race Is On   When buying a UPS, don't forget to factor in the time it takes to physically travel to your server. And consider that in the event of a power failure—it might be dark! It might be wise to keep a flashlight handy.

A UPS is not the device to skimp on and save money. Invest in a well-built, powerful UPS. During the first thunderstorm, you will make your money back.

 Self Shut Down   Today's UPS's almost always feature the capability to gracefully shut down your server in case the power goes out and you are not available. Ensure you buy a UPS that supports this feature, but more importantly, make sure you implement this feature.

RAID ARRAY

The most exposure you will have to disasters in a Microsoft Exchange 5.5 Server installation is hard drive errors. After all, these mechanical devices see a lot of wear and tear. Microsoft Exchange 5.5 is a transaction-based software package and uses the hard drive storage space heavily. Almost constantly, in fact, Microsoft Exchange 5.5 is reading and writing to disk through the use of transaction logs. One disk error, and your whole Microsoft Exchange 5.5 installation could crash.

Luckily, there is an inexpensive method of preventing a disk error from wiping out your Microsoft Exchange 5.5 installation. RAID can provide the safety net you need.

RAID allows you to use multiple drives as one. To provide fault tolerance and disaster prevention, you need to format your RAID drive. The most common RAID *levels* are 1 or 5. Levels relate to the method in which you want data written to the RAID.

Level 1 is the most simplistic form or redundancy, but is also the most costly. Commonly referred to as *mirroring*, Level 1 uses a 1:1 disk ratio to store data. For example, if you were using four 2-gigabyte drives with Level 1, you wouldn't have a total capacity of 8 gigabytes, you would have 4 gigabytes. Why? Each primary drive being used for storage needs an identical secondary drive assigned to it to keep a mirror image of what is written to the primary drive.

Level 5 is the most common RAID level used today. It provides something called *data striping with parity*. Instead of using a 1:1 disk ratio, it uses a 1:3 to 1:32 ratio where all the drives are used for redundancy. Each drive has a part of the other drives on it. If any of the drives fails in the RAID, the others pick up for it.

Mirroring   With striping, one of the most common methods of bringing fault tolerance to your data storage is creating a duplicate copy of your data on other partitions or drives. For instance, if you have a 9-gigabyte disk drive you are using as storage, you can add another 9 gigabyte drive and instruct Windows NT Server to mirror the drives. Any changes made to the first drive are made to the second drive, thus creating a perfect copy.

Striping   Some users find disk mirroring a waste of drive space because you need twice the amount of drive space. Another method of fault tolerance is data striping with parity. Data striping uses multiple disks of the same size in a set. Instead of creating a duplicate copy of the data, the data is written to the set multiple times and creates a parity bit. The parity bit is used to re-create one of the drives in case of a failure. As an example, if you are using four 9-gigabyte drives in your server, mirroring would only allow you to use 18 gigabytes of storage instead of all 36 gigabytes. Disk striping with parity allows you to use 27 gigabytes of storage. The extra 9 gigabytes are used for the parity bit.

Using RAID is a must in today's high availability servers. Look for a RAID array that supports the capability to *hot-swap* a drive if it goes bad. Hot swapping allows you to replace the drive without bringing the server down.

SOFTWARE DISASTER PREVENTION

When you think of disaster prevention, do you really think of software as being capable of helping? In the past there was little software could do to aid in disaster prevention.

In today's world of servers though, there are two software-related items that can prevent disasters from occurring:

* Clustering
* Hot fixes

CLUSTERING

Sometimes in computing, what's old becomes new again. This is what happened with clustering. A staple of the 1970s minicomputer installation, clustering is now making a comeback as the ultimate disaster prevention tool.

Clustering is a group of independent servers managed as a single system for fault tolerance and other benefits. Each of the servers in a cluster has its own processor, memory, and NIC card, but there is a shared RAID array or mirrored drives for data.

Connected via a network cable, the clustered servers are continuously aware of what the other is doing. In the case of a total server shutdown, the other server in the cluster begins to service the downed server's clients. The clients will experience a brief period of being unable to access the network, but they can continue to work as normal as soon as the cutover to the remaining server is made.

The software for clustering control updates each server as to what the other server is currently doing.

Clustering is a good solution for companies that need high availability and minimal data loss.

HOT FIXES

Microsoft periodically releases hot fixes to address critical bugs found in Microsoft Exchange 5.5. The hot fixes are released before the more common Service Pack is released.

You should, at least monthly, check Microsoft's FTP site for the release of hot fixes. A benefit of using one of the world's more popular email solutions is that other users might encounter critical system errors before you do. To ensure you are protected against security issues, you should implement security related hot fixes as they become available. You should implement other fixes only if you are experiencing the particular problem. Be aware that applying a hot fix might cause other problems because they are not fully tested by Microsoft.

 Visit the FTP Site Microsoft's FTP location for Microsoft Exchange 5.5 hot fixes is `ftp://ftp.microsoft.com/bussys/exchange/exchange-public/fixes/Eng/Exchg5.5/`.

Whatever you do, *never* install a hot fix blindly on your Microsoft Exchange 5.5 installation. You should test the hot fix on a test server on your test network first.

By taking these steps, you can ensure your Microsoft Exchange 5.5 Server is as disaster-proof as possible.

In this lesson you learned how to prevent disasters using environment, hardware, and software methods.

INDEX